I0133226

Jack's Winning Words

John H. Freed and Friends

Jack's Winning Words

© 2014 John H. Freed

ISBN-13:

9780692025284 (SFLToday.org)

ISBN-10:

0692025286

This edition (or subsequent revisions) will remain available on Amazon.com indefinitely unless Jack asks me to remove it. I have set the price to the lowest allowed by Amazon.

The painting on the cover (based on Jack's Blogger profile) is from friend of SFL, Amy Sellers Artist in Mt. Dora, Florida (amysellersart.com). I have sent the original oil painting to Jack.

Published by Stewardship for Life | SFLToday.org

Foreword

For several years now I have received a weekday morning email containing Jack's Winning Words. I decided to publish (through Stewardship for Life) four months of Jack's blog (without editing) for his friends but mostly as a gift to Jack. I know Jack discussed creating a book of his Winning Words a few years ago. There is a great joy as an author holding your first published book. It is nowhere near as wonderful as holding your child for the first time, but nevertheless a memorable moment.

Even readers that do not receive Jack's weekday updates by email can quickly get a flavor of Jack's optimistic and friendly messages, as well as his readers' responses (also unedited). You will notice he gives each respondent a nickname (mine is GOOD DEBT JON), and he directs his responses to those names. A few others are: TARMART REV, PEPPERMINT MARY, ES IN COLORADO, FM IN WISCONSIN, ES IN MICHIGAN, CK IN MICHIGAN, FACEBOOK LIZ, MICHIZONA RAY, BS IN ENGLAND, PH IN MINNESOTA, RI IN BOSTON, SHARIN' SHARON, PLAIN FOLKS CHESTER, BLAZING OAKS, PH IN MINNESOTA, INDY GENIE, YOOPER BOB. HONEST JOHN, JT IN MINNESOTA, BBC IN ILLINOIS, DR J IN OHIO, OUTHOUSE JUDY, TAMPA SHIRL, SBP IN FLORIDA, TERI GIANETTI, DMF IN MINNESOTA, JAN IN CALIFORNIA, WATERFORD JAN, RB IN MICHIGAN, TRIHARDER, PH IN MESA, HAPPY TRAILS IN NOVA SCOTIA, LP IN PLYMOUTH, HCC CHUCK, RS IN TEXAS, HS IN ILLINOIS, or whatever "handle" he has given you. (There are more, I did not try to include them all, sorry if you got left out).

Part of the brilliance of the blog is the way Jack (intentionally or not) misuses the platform. He posts answers or responses to emails right in the body of the blog with his initial comments. From my point of view this is far more useful to readers than clicking to see a response on a separate page (there are a few responses on the separate pages that I did not include). The purpose of a blog is communication, not conformity, and I believe the way Jack is using the platform is far better than the way it was intended.

I was introduced to Jack by Lynn Kirkby back in 2003 or 2004 when I was writing my book *Good Debt, Bad Debt* (Penguin, 2005, 2007). Lynn thought we would hit it off well, and from my perspective I think we did. I finally had the pleasure of meeting Jack, 'toe-to-toe', at a Farmington Hills, Michigan Starbucks in late 2013. He was as gracious and kind in person as he is in print.

No one I can think of is more dedicated to his **Congregation Without Walls** than Jack. Most people retire and never engage again with the people they once served... (eg: my former pastor went fishing in 1992 and has not been heard from since). Jack not only stays engaged, but takes on new projects like me; a sarcastic Irish-Norwegian-Libertarian-Southern Baptist, skeptical of all things political.

I have spent much of my life seeking to matter. Matter to myself and others. There is much to be admired and modeled in the life of John H. Freed, both in public service and the lives of his family. According to author Brendon Burchard, in *Life's Golden Ticket*, the questions we all have at the end of life are: 1. Did I Live? 2. Did I Love? 3. Did I Matter? I think Brendon's questions are excellent. I have seen too many friends having to answer these questions too soon (at least too soon for me). When the time comes for Pastor Jack, the answers will have to bring a smile to his face.

Jack, I cannot speak for all of your subscribers. Yet I suspect without exception they would all agree that in our lives you have definitely mattered. The daily digital encouragement provided has meant a great deal to me over the years. Above all you make us think. You send a quote or a phrase with a bit of commentary, and let us, your readers, figure it out. And for that simple act, many of us are truly indebted.

Jon Hanson

April, 2014

Below is a back and forth between Lynn Kirkby and Jack (I asked Lynn to get the information on when Winning Words began!).   I hope they will both forgive me for making this private communication public (already read by the NSA anyway).

--- From: Lynn Sent: Thursday, February 27, 2014 12:32 PM To: jhfreed27@comcast.net Subject: Re: Winning Words m

Hi Jack! Yesterday it was very good to visit once again with Jon Hanson. He and I had not been in touch in some time.

We agreed that WINNING WORDS has taken on a life of its own, as it were. For a very long time now (when did you begin this effort?), WW has served as a continuing source of engagement both for mind and heart. It is certain that your readers, family and friends alike, have come to anticipate WW as a regular and most valuable form of soul food, sustaining and encouraging all of us to live on in ways meaningful and helpful to others. Whatever your initial intent with the first daily "publication" of WINNING WORDS, your enterprise has proven the highest friendship to many.

THANK YOU!

Lynn

P.S. Our prayers are with you, Mary and your entire family always.

Reply to Lynn from Jack:

Winning Words got its start in 1992 with the gift of a computer disc from Daughter Jeanne. It was full of positive messages. I began sharing a few of them with family and friends...who suggested that I forward them to others. Slow, but sure, it grew. It now numbers about 400 who receive them. I post some responses (anonymously) on a blog. An internet "newspaper," West Bloomfield Patch, also posts them. One of the reasons I enjoy getting up at 5 am, is that I can sit down at my computer and set out the day's words. I call the people who receive them...C-WOW, my Congregation With Out Walls.

Friday, November 29, 2013

Jack's Winning Words 11/28/13

"Do not wait. The time will never be just right!" (Napoleon Hill) I read of a man in Ohio who set up a tent outside of a Best Buy store last Monday at 5 am, in order to be 1st in line on Black Friday. Not just today, but every day is a time to decide what's most important in life. Thanksgiving is really a time to puts things into perspective. A friend told me that at their Thanksgiving table, each one stated what they were thankful for. Her little grand-daughter said, "Brown sugar." That's what thanks-giving means..   ;-) Jack

FROM PH IN MINNESOTA: (Received at 6 am) hey, have you become an insomniac? go back to bed.
====JACK: I slept in today and didn't get up until 5:01 am, so I missed being first in line at Walmart..

FROM LS IN MICHIGAN: ...responding to your words this morning - I am thankful for your writings each day to look forward to and to begin my day w a prayer, expressing my grateful appreciation at being granted another day . Your words present the basis for a moment to reflect and process what you choose to bring into my life each morning - I enjoy being w you each morning so thank you for doing your work w integrity and passion ====JACK: Thanksgiving ought to be observed more than once a year. How about once a day? Each morning, as I send out Winning Words, I'm thankful for being able to be in computer touch with my friends.

FROM TARMART REV: Always thankful for family and friends ====JACK: ...and the opportunity for you to do ministry in a variety of ways.

FROM RI IN BOSTON: The WW make a lot of sense...don't wait, do it! My wife's attitude is "get to it."   Whether she thinks about baking something, or sewing something, or cleaning out the closets, she doesn't hesitate and it gets done. I on the other hand have a habit of putting things off...until the weekend, or next week or? Relating that with the matter of "thanks-giving", I have a story of my personal disappointment. A few years ago I saw a news item about an accomplished man who had helped me significantly when I was studying at the university. I realized I should write him, to thank him for the interest he had shown in me, and how it had been so beneficial to my future. I decided to do it, and someone I knew provided his address at a university in California. With that I was prepared to write...but I waited. Just a couple weeks later the man's obituary was published. Due to my procrastination he never learned how valuable his help had been to me. ====JACK: In 2 Timothy 4 there's a poignant account of Paul writing to young Timothy. Paul is in prison (probably in Rome). He wants Timothy to visit him and bring a cloak (it's cold in the cell) and his scrolls (he wants to read), and, most of all, Timothy himself (Paul is lonesome). He adds: "Come before winter." If Timothy delays, he will have to wait until spring when the sailing season resumes. We don't know if he caught the last ship, or not. We don't know if he ever made it before Paul died. But, if he didn't, he probably uttered and reuttered a regret..."If only...." ====RI: Your comment about Timothy needing to sail before Winter, or be stuck until Spring, takes me back to my travels in Turkey in 1964. I was in Istanbul the end of September and made plans to go south to visit Ephesus, and to get there required crossing the Sea of Marmara. I went to the harbor on Monday and booked a ticket on the ferry departing on Tuesday. Tuesday morning I awoke and looked out of my hotel at rain and heavy winds. When I got to the ferry landing, waves were blowing up over the docks, and all travel was cancelled. The sea was wild. Wednesday the weather calmed down enough that the ferry decided to make the crossing. I was hesitant but did it. With the vessels and gear they had in Paul's day, I can imagine the risk of being at sea in foul weather. BTW, Thanks for the text source of Paul writing to Timothy, and your explanation of what was happening then. While looking into the text myself I found information that Timothy was very dear to Paul, and because Timothy's mother was Jewish while his father was Greek, Paul circumcised Timothy to affirm he was a Jew, and thus preclude Timothy being persecuted by the Jews.

FROM GOOD DEBT JON: As I often say, "Hesitation, procrastination, contemplation, more waitin' cannot build a nation. *Perspective is elective.*" One of my favorites is the late Shel Silverstein, "All those should, ought, and musts-- run and hid; from one little did."====JACK: I've always enjoyed Shel's writings and cartoons, but your reference to him caused me to look further into his life. "Laughing on the outside and crying on the inside" seems to apply to Shel and his family. Most of us create a protective around our personal life.====JON: Oh, BTW, if you read Samuel Smiles (Scottish) you can see a lot of where Napoleon Hill came from. His books *Self Help* and *Thrift* were precursors to many of the more famous American writers.====JACK: "Smiles" is a good name for someone who's a motivations speaker/writer....

FROM JM IN MICHIGAN: It is reportedly Martin Luther who said, "How soon "Not now' becomes never." Same message as today's quote -- and I need to remember these because I am a huge procrastinator.====JACK: I have a sign on my wall..."If it weren't for the last minute, a lot of things wouldn't get done."

FROM ES IN COLORADO: I like that little granddaughter. I think I'm thankful for brown sugar too!
How are things in your neck of the wood, Jack?====JACK: The thing I liked about that little girl...She was honest about what she was thankful. Sometimes "the older folks" say what seems to be appropriate. Of course, when they say, "I'm thankful for my health," I guess that's appropriate, too. I wouldn't expect them to say, "Brown sugar!"

FROM BS IN ENGLAND: It is my life.====JACK: The twists and turns of life make it both interesting and exciting. Thanks for being a part of mine.

FROM FM IN WISCONSIN: I received a telephone call yesterday from a pastor in Minnesota with whom I worked many years.   Ralph said he was in church on Wednesday evening, and the pastor at St. Andrews in his sermon asked the worshippers to think about a person who has been a significant help to them in life and call them on the phone to thank them on Thanksgiving.   So I received a call yesterday – which was a great gift from this thoughtful pastor.   Ralph did not wait and the time was so right.   I have so much for which to be thankful – especially for so many pastors who carried out the mission of the church so effectively – like a pastor who moved Illinois to Orchard Lake, MI.====JACK: What a great suggestion by that St. Andrews pastor! Sometimes people actually do listen to sermons and follow up on them...more often than not. I thank God for many people who have influenced me.

FROM JK IN CALIFORNIA: for fun... it's true... :) timing is never perfect ... to execute! JuSt Do it!!====JACK: I like "Send In the Clowns," especially the part about "timing." Timing is so important in many areas of life.

FROM SBP IN FLORIDA: For me, every day is a "thanks" giving day! WW has helped me delve into myself and I appreciate and value the daily thought-provoking sermonettes. Thank!...you. I'm reading The Christmas Spirit by Joel Osteen. (Picked it up at WalMart) What a good feeling it evokes in me! Thank you John/Jack for the WWs which stimulate my thinking and generates introspection. (I think I've said this before.) ====JACK: Many things, days, events, people can cause introspection. One of the most ancient of proverbs is attributed to Socrates, "Know thyself!" When you "get a handle" on self, you are on the way toward getting a handle on other things that are happening in your life.====SBP: And Shakespeare... a father to son..."This above all, to thine own self be true." ====JACK: In order to be true to yourself, you have to know yourself...and sometimes that "knowing" depends upon what other see and relate back.
====SBP: This came to mind..."Know then thyself, presume not God to scan; The proper study of mankind is man." ====JACK: I'm impressed. In what context did you come across The Essay On Man?

Wednesday, November 27, 2013

Jack's Winning Words 11/27/13

"I pledge allegiance to the Earth and all the life which it supports, one planet, in our care, irreplaceable, with sustenance and respect for all." (Jessica Lamb) Tomorrow is that day when we usually recount what it is that we're thankful for. Try making a list, using the word, T-H-A-N-K-S-G-I-V-I-N-G, as an acrostic. T could stand for "turkey." God is great! God is good! We have so many things for which to give thanks. ;-) Jack

 FROM TS IN MICHIGAN: Exceptional====JACK: I wondered how it might be "taken" when I sent it out. Thanks for being the "first responder."

 FROM GOOD DEBT JON: Poetically, Thanksgiving says it all as a word, both noun and verb. A personal acrostic: Three (the family God gave me), Humbleness, Action (if we are the body), Nondenominational, Kindness (even where fondness does not exist), Grace, Insight, Virtue (or victory), Incomplete (without giving thanks), Noon (when church is done) Grace (worth repeating). Thanksgiving has always been a special day for me. I can remember our family (after Dad died) receiving the food baskets from the firemen or the local church folks. How striking it was to be delivering similar help to others in my 20's with my wife and still 40 plus years later. Around here it is Thanksgiving that prepares our hearts for Christmas. We will have around 25 to 30 again this year and if you are near Etna, Ohio you are welcome, we will have family, waitresses, Barista's, friends, soldiers, and who ever we meet today. I prefer

Christmas with family but Thanksgiving means fellowship (Baptist code word for eating). Have a great day Pastor Jack. ====JACK: What a great family story that you have shared on this Thanksgiving Eve. Thank you! Thanks, too, for taking the time to do the acrostic. Maybe I should sit down and work one out. A lot of times we give advice, but forget to look in the mirror.

 FROM PEPPERMINT MARY: we learn this pledge at school during the month of april in honor of earth day. first we say the pledge of allegiance to our flag, then the earth pledge to the globe. some of the little ones look at us like we are nuts, changing things up like that!...oh, and, i'm thankful for you and your winning words!====JACK: I think I'll try that pledge with a group of adults to see what their reaction might be. Stay tooned!

 FROM FM IN WISCONSIN: And the H stands for Hats Off – hats off to Jack Freed and his daily WW's.   Much to be thankful for! EVERYDAY!====JACK: K is for Kindness that is shown. Thanks.

 FROM JE IN MICHIGAN: Here's my list:
Time off to spend with my family!
Home, husband and health.
Animals, especially Baxter our dog.
Nancy and Ben, my parents.
Kindness that is shown to myself and others.
Sisters and brothers and my whole family.
God and my faith.

Interest in so many things, the news, my vocation/profession, gardening, films, crafts, art, etc......

Victory for the bond and for the WLC Marching Band.

Involvement in decisions at work and invitations from friends to fun events.

Nieces and nephews and my whole family!!!

Giving -- the ability to be in a position to be able to give to others.

This was a great exercise .... it made think about the many things I am thankful for.

====JE: Jack, I made an important revision .... can't forget my husband ....Thankfulness abounds,

====JACK: That's a great list, especially with the revision.

 FROM BLAZING OAKS: I had nev er seen this pledge, but it is appropriate for this season of the year! Reinforces my recycling intent!---Looks like we will be 43 at the OAKS Celebration, and we will all express thanks for something special to us tomorrow. I'm sure it will run the gamut of T-H-A-N -K-S-G-I-V-I-N-G. We are so blessed! Even tho we have to remember such dear ones in the family no longer clasping hands in the "Thankful Circle"...plus "the others."====JACK: 43? That's a really, really BIG circle....plus "the others."   I'm reminded of the old country hymn..."Will the circle be unbroken By and by, Lord, by and by There's a better home a-waiting In the sky, Lord, in the sky In the sky, Lord, in the sky " You can sing the part of Mother Maybelle Carter. Strum the autoharp, if you have one

 FROM SHARIN' SHARON: Hi, JE stimulated me to also think of a list:

T rust that God always seems to give me

H ope

A-ngels--both here on earth among us and in heaven

N-ormal days--not terribly exciting but I'm EXTREMELY thankful they're still coming at my age

K-indness and mercy

S-haring which I always hope to learn to do better and for which I am grateful for others who do

G-od who gives faith to JE and me too

I-nclusiveness - DIVERSITY is wonderful!!!!

V-oice to sing and tell the story of how good God is to us, taking care of us all the time

I-nner peace

N-ice warm house, coat, gloves, scarf and hugs

G-race

and bonn appetite--enjoy your Thanksgiving celebration meal!!!!!

====JACK: Yours is also an excellent list, including some that I wouldn't have thought of.

FROM JT IN MINNESOTA: As always thanks for your words of wisdom. David remains in the care center and is failing, but is resilient and who knows what the future holds. As we went around the table naming what we are thankful for including family, friends, faith and so on my little grand daughter said, "I'm Thankful for brown sugar!" It was refreshing and surprising.====JACK: Brown sugar? That's why kids are so much fun. When we went around the table filling in the acrostic, THANKSGIVING, for the letter I, my son used the word, intestines. Without them, we couldn't enjoy our meal. :

Tuesday, November 26, 2013

Jack's Winning Words 11/26/13

"I believe that having a spiritual life is so important in everybody's life." (Lou Holtz) Many people these days see themselves as "spiritual" as over against "religious." Isn't it possible to be both...in tune with God...and, at the same time, working with others to do the "Godly" thing? Coach Holtz has a way of giving pep talks that make his listeners think. What does it mean for you to have a spiritual/religious life?   ;-) Jack

 FROM MICHIZONA RAY: Everyone who has life has a spirit; hence, everyone is also spiritual. It's really quite an obvious and unnecessary comment for one to claim that one is "spiritual". It would be equally unnecessary to claim that one is physical. Rather, the valuable comment is to how one engages one's spirituality (which is more likely what he means). Religion (to trace back, to connect with) provides one the opportunity for the re-enactment of the story, or to bring life to it, through the ritual for the purpose of "communing" with the God of one's theology. In Christian theology (Jesus is Lord) I utilize the Lutheran religion in our community. When not with the rest of the congregation, I remain a part of the Body of Christ, in concert with the rest of the Body of Christ. Hence, we don't "go to church", we are the Church. Where we go the Church goes...and so does the Spirit. Yes, spirituality is important indeed. So, I guess Lou Holtz's comment is really quite an understatement isn't it? ====JACK: Cutting to the chase...I think Lou is saying that everyone should have a place for God in his/her life.

FROM HONEST JOHN: "The Spiritual Dimension of Life" was the title of my keynote speech for the recent Michigan Stephen Ministry Network Convention.   It was well received and folks wanted me to publish it.   I am working on polishing it up right now.   If I like the result, I may try to publish it====JACK: You and Lou seem to be coaches on the same page. He's been a football coach, and you've been a debate coach.

FROM TARMART REV: I'm sure there are still many in the making . . . but at my age, I'm missing many of my hero's from yesteryears gone by.====JACK: You don't have to wait until Thursday to give thanks for them.

FROM FACEBOOK LIZ: "Religious" connotes church-going, is my interpretation... spiritual is in touch with God. BTW, I love Lou Holtz! ====JACK: Ideally, church should be a place where one can be in touch with God, but that is not always the case. Jesus found it necessary to cleanse the Temple. The Spirit of God can be in a box, but does not have to be confined to the box.====LIZ: The spirit of God is everywhere!

FROM IKE AT THE MIC: I believe you then can truly enjoy a successful balanced life because you are then able to "walk the talk"====JACK: When you lose your balance, you're apt to fall...and then all kinds of complications set it...especially when you're on the other side of 50.

FROM SHARIN' SHARON: I know so many people--both family and friends-- for which "religious" seems to be a word which connotes something very limited. Actually, I sense they think of religion only in terms of law and churches only as a place where you are told about the laws and that you should be a lawful people. The word "spiritual" seems to them more something they can grasp as being helpful in their lives--for example one friend told me that for her God "is everywhere"--seems that the God she knows is spiritually everywhere but is not necessarily spiritually in church but she thinks is religiously there and not really drawing her to go be there with Him, maybe because of all of His laws and the crappy people there who are likely to be so judgmental. I have some people who keep putting on my Facebook that the Ten Commandments need to be posted in public buildings and prayer needs to be in schools and God needs to be on our money and so forth and so forth but I believe we need to pay the greatest attention to law/Gospel in our churches and help people to come closer to God in receiving the whole message--the Pastor just doesn't do it through the sermons, somehow every single worshipper has to be a little priest and figure out how to talk to people and be with people so they see we embody that tension of law/Gospel ourselves and have a believable and authentic religion. Help religion to become a positive word for people who think it's just laws and ritual. Thanks--I needed to try to think this through some more today.====JACK: Sadly, some churches (pastors and people) have misused and misinterpreted "the Spirit." And, sometimes, "listeners" have missed the message, but God has a way of getting around those obstacles, and that's what "Spirituality" seeks to accomplish. It's a personal thing...God reaching into the soul of the individual. I'm comfortable with letting God do his job, while I try my best to do mine.====SHARON: Enjoyed SBP and your commentary. Just heard from our Pastor's sermon last Sunday, upon the 60th anniversary of our congregation, that it isn't like it used to be--the Pastor at the beginning of the forming of the congregation said his job was to step aside because the people were just flowing in and the main thing was not to put any hindrances to them. Now, we need to go outside and do all kinds of "outreach" and be not only spiritual and religious but busy (Pastor also said some things will succeed, some will fail) but I must say I'm somewhat stuck on not putting any hindrances to people when they come because have seen quite a bit of the revolving door church these last decades. The sermon at the Cathelic church next door this noon was pay attention to the Stations of the Cross and confession and being merciful, not scolding anyone, when people came to Jesus, he never scolded anyone. That makes a lot of sense to me but walking home I reflected upon how much Jesus scolded the synagogue of His day. There is no other option than to put my trust in God and believing the Church will survive no matter how much any one of us don't know what we're doing. It is sort of easier to be a gentle peaceful Christian worshipping in a church where you don't know anything much about the struggles they are going through to stay open. Just saying. Thanks, especially, your enhanced commentary on the relationship between spirituality and religiousity.

 FROM SBP IN FLORIDA: For me, spiritual and religious do not walk "hand in hand". They are intermingled/blended with religion shaping and reshaping the spiritual....the spiritual evolving and affecting my thoughts, words and deeds. And I'm still churning this WW.

Thanks.====JACK: Theologians have "churned" over this for ages. I've come to the conclusion that "spirituality" is our one on one relationship with the Spirit (God...Ultimate Being) and religion is when like-minded spiritual people come together to better express their God-relationship.

FROM JE IN MICHIGAN: What it means for me to have a spiritual/religious life is to live life in a giving, joyous way as to consider others first. Actually, I'm happiest when I'm helping someone else. I am so thankful this Thanksgiving for the passage of our school district's bond, for my family, faith, friends and for my job. I'm thankful for my job because it allows me, of course to be able to pay my bills, but it also affords me so many opportunities to give of myself in so many ways to others.====JACK: Yes, we have much for which to be thankful.

FROM PLAIN FOLKS CHESTER: This one confuses me. How can you lead a religious life and not a spiritual one?====JACK: Jesus said (in the Sermon on the Mount): "Not everyone who says to me, 'Lord, Lord,' will enter the kingdom of heaven, but only the one who does the will of my Father who is in heaven."

FROM BLAZING OAKS: I believe that a spiritual life is essential for any deep meaning to our lives; but some who never seem to introspect, just "go along", day after day, don't even realize what they're missing, at least to outward appearances. I'm sure there are some deeply spiritual people who don't practice "religion" in a church, too. But a relationship with the Almighty God gives meaning to all of life, both mountain top and valley experiences. "Believing is Seeing" as Bill titled one sermon....it is true!====JACK: Whether the spiritual relationship with God is "deep" is not dependent upon what "we" do. The power is the Spirit's power. "Behold, I tell you a mystery." Spirituality is mysterious.

FROM CWR IN MICHIGAN: I think that contingent upon place of Birth, "Rearing", Cultural and Ethnic enviornment, Education, and as well as Family practices....that the "idea of God" takes on many and diverse forms.even within established institutional religious organizations......and is fluid.....no matter how "doctrinal " the influences are. .....and I think that spiritual /religious life Is ALWAYS fluid and ,by nature, transitional....that is, evolving.. Frankly, Doctrinal Rigidity is unfortunate. Doctrine is a form of intellectual organization, is not only fluid but is also situational. I think that perhaps one of the greatest advances in Evangelical progression was the invention of the Telephone the typewriter and the eraser.....and that a spiritual/religious life is the precurser of Evolution.......personal and cultural.   . Cheers!====JACK: Jack Pearl, an old-time radio comedian, would tell far-fetched stories, and his partner would express skepticism and say, "Vas you dere, Sharlie?" One of the reasons we call our religious beliefs, "faith," is because we have to rely on what others tell us. Sharlie vasn't dere. I'm satisfied with that.

FROM JR IN CALIFORNIA: God seems to keep my head above water. :Your not too bad at that yourself.====JACK: I see too many things that happen in life that seem to be more than coincidences. I believe in the spiritual presence of God...and I find comfort in that.

FROM KZB IN COLORADO: Go Lou!!! Lou said a really funny thing at the pep rally for the national championship - he talked about how he had the chaplain come in to pray for the team, and the chaplain said, "you know Lou, Jesus doesn't care who wins..." Lou said, "I know father, but his MOTHER does." ====JACK: Was he the football coach when you were at Notre Dame? I always liked to see that little guy prancing along the sideline. He's a great motivational speaker, too.

FROM PEPPERMINT MARY: i think that believing in the spiritual realm is the foundation. choosing or not choosing a religion in the human realm is the path that one follows to honor spirit.====JACK: It's hard to believe in something that you can't see. A sheet was thrown over Casper so that we could see the ghost (spirit). God threw a sheet (Jesus) over the Spirit in order that we could "see" Him (God).

Monday, November 25, 2013

Jack's Winning Words 11/25/13

"When you're tempted to react in the same old way, ask if you want to be a prisoner of the past, or a pioneer of the future." (Deepak Chopra) Futurists are predicting some amazing things...robotic maids, flying cars, healthful food in a pill. There are "luddites" who react negatively to stuff like that. I suppose most of us are moderates. We like some of the past, but accept that the future has a way of becoming the present.   ;-) Jack

FROM HONEST JOHN: I love the past. I love the present. I look forward to the future.   Why be one dimensional?====JACK: You probably like 3-D movies, too.

 FROM TARMART REV: From the time we are born, cycled in and out of changes . . . .was here before we arrived and will be present still when we say farewell Planet Earth!!!====JACK: You and I are part of the change. Here today and gone tomorrow.====REV: Hopefully able to stop along the way and smell a few roses.====JACK: This week I hope to smell the turkey as it's cooking.

 FROM RI IN BOSTON: Well you know, Deepak, the reverse of that is possible too. I sometimes feel I was a pioneer of the past but am now becoming a prisoner of the future.====JACK: That's a good thought. BTW, I've never been a prisoner in jail, except one time....when I was locked up as part of a Muscular Dystrophy fund-raiser. I didn't get out until people paid my bail with donations.

 FROM MICHIZONA RAY: The temporal realm certainly brings its challenges to man. Living or attempting to relive the past has no true present or future; but a life of fantasy. In a true sense, the future never occurs because the present is as close as we can get to it. And, the present comes and goes into the past as soon as we experience it. I wonder what eternity must be like --- all three simultaneously?====JACK: The present immediately becomes the past, and the future never happens. Or...Is the past, present and future all a fantasy?====RAY: You have tapped into the issue at hand: the delicate distinctions among our many experiences...How much of what we experience is "true" and how much is "reality"? What is true is true for itself. What is real is by my own determination; but what is real is not necessarily true.====JACK: Some children have fun playing with their imaginary friends. Adults can have fantasies, too.

FROM BLAZING OAKS: A Robotic Cleaning lady would be most welcome at my house today, as I gear up for 41 Thanksgiving guests!! But of course think of all the aids we have that would have seemed heavenly to housewives 150 yrs. ago, like vacuum sweepers, diswashers, et all. Guess I can't complain. And the future looks to be awesome with fantastic discoveries and inventions that amaze us! But food in a pill will never taste and smell as delicious, as what we have now. HMMM I an smell that turkey already!! ====JACK: 41 is really a crowd to have around the table. Jesus only has 13.

FROM SBP IN FLORIDA: We're a solution comprised of the past as we blend into the present as we are infused into the future as we....As I churn today's WW....lots of aspects to think about....Thanks. ====JACK: Nobody has asked about "luddite." I think that it's such an interesting word...with a fascinating story behind it.====SBP: My assumption was/is that everybody but me had a base of reference. So....I "Googled" the word.....and it is an interesting , meaningful word. Worthy of more conjecture. My grandson and I were discussing the origins of language this weekend. How has it evolved from "grunts" to syntax> WW just stirs up..... ====JACK: Grandsons are fun...I have 4. Granddaughters are also good to interact with...2 of them.

Friday, November 22, 2013

Jack's Winning Words 11/22/13

"No matter how tall the mountain, it cannot block out the sun." (Chinese Proverb) Something I enjoy about flying is when the plane breaks through the clouds into bright sunlight. A friend would often quote, Longfellow's "Rainy Day" poem. "The day is cold and dark and dreary...Be still, sad heart!...Behind the clouds is the sun still shining." Some days may be dark for you and me. But, rainy days aren't forever!   ;-) Jack

RAINY DAY by Henry Wadsworth Longfellow
 The day is cold, and dark, and dreary;
It rains, and the wind is never weary;
The vine still clings to the mouldering wall,
But at every gust the dead leaves fall,
And the day is dark and dreary.

My life is cold, and dark, and dreary;
It rains, and the wind is never weary;
My thoughts still cling to the mouldering Past,
But the hopes of youth fall thick in the blast,
And the days are dark and dreary.

Be still, sad heart! and cease repining;
Behind the clouds is the sun still shining;

Thy fate is the common fate of all,

Into each life some rain must fall,

Some days must be dark and dreary.

FROM MICHIZONA RAY: We have been studying the Psalms recently, and this reminds me of a prevailing theme that portrays the rainy and dark times of what seems to the psalmist as God's forsaking his chosen people. They ask "for how much longer" will Your absence of favor last. I suppose there is always "Son-shine" in heaven; while the things of the world "cloud" our regular access to the warmth of His favor. ====JACK: The Book of Ecclesiastes says that there's a time for everything...to live and to die..to laugh and to cry...for rainy days and sunny days. It's raining outside today, but tomorrow the sun will shine. ====RAY: It's usually sunny here! Thankfully!====JACK: You can't drink sunshine.====RAY: True; but you can bathe in it!

FROM HONEST JOHN: Sometimes it seems like some of those big semis on the road block out the sun.   Always glad to get away from them....but soon his cousin is there to do the job.====JACK: My brother-in-law had a VW hippie bus and would tailgate semis, believing that he'd get better gas mileage that way.

FROM PEPPERMINT MARY: there is a great children's book entitled, "ming lo moves the mountain". i think you'd like it!====JACK: Does it have pictures and big print?

FROM IKE AT THE MIC: Great message! you should present that as invocation at an Optimist Club breakfast meeting...."The world of achievement has always belonged to the optimist".. ====JACK: I really like the Longfellow poem. He did good work!

 FROM TAMPA SHIRL: Always an optimist. It seems there are always breakthroughs. I am taking two course at OLLI at USF. One is about DNA- way out of my comfort zone , and the other is about the Civil War. The DNA class is held in a new USF School of Medicine in down town Tampa where they teach about robotic medicine. The Civil War teacher blows my mind with all of his knowledge and presentations. He is a real Civil War buff and makes everything so interesting with his power pioints and maps.One thing that I have noticed, though,.I am getting to be the oldest in all of my classes, even though I don't feel old. The rest of the class is now of the Viet Nam era.====JACK: Civil War buffs only know second-hand information. Don't worry about being the oldest. As long as you've got all your marbles, you can still be in the game.

 FROM RI IN BOSTON: Ah yes, that radiant sun, how it lifts our spirit. There's so much drama when the darkness of a summer storm passes and bright sunshine suddenly breaks through. Flying above the clouds as you described is a special experience. Like Longfellow, the poet Radcliffe Squires saw the beauty above the clouds too: "I see how the cloud bank is really a landscape where sunlight makes rainbows. I see white valleys whose white streams flow into snow meadows where pearly cattle drift. I see pale mountains where ghostly eagles fly." There is so much of wonder all around us that we generally fail to recognize. It's raining in Boston today...but not forever!====JACK: What differentiates our planet from others (and makes it habitable) is the rain and the sunshine...in just the right amount.

FROM TARMART REV: Another good word to begin my day with!!====JACK: Did you ever sing this song?

Climb, climb up sunshine mountain

Heavenly breezes blow;

Climb, climb up sunshine mountain

Faces all aglow.

Turn, turn from sin and doubting,

Look to God on high,

Climb, climb up sunshine mountain

You and I.

====REV: That and "This little light of mine, I'm gonna let it shine!"

FROM CS IN WISCONSIN: Think this really applies to me lately. Had knee replacement surgery on Oct. 28th, with complications.   Thing are getting better, but it takes time. I'm looking forward to the sunshine after all the cloudy miserable days!!!!====JACK: Do you remember when people, who weren't feeling well, would say, "I got the miseries!"? Sorry about your miseries. "The Doctor" says: "Try reading Longfellow's poem again."

FROM RP & CP IN FLORIDA: Thank you. We needed that today.===JACK: "Look for the Silver Lining" is more than just a good song.

FROM NORM, THE REALTOR: Inspired by your post this morning -
====JACK: A ray of sunshine breaks through the clouds on this day. Thanks.

FROM JR IN CALIFORNIA: YOU ARE SUCH A UPPER FOR ME.====JACK: A Chinese Proverb and a Longfellow poem and the Holy Spirit of God make "the magic" happen.

FROM KF IN MICHIGAN: The winter solstice is in 4 weeks, which means after that the days (daylight) will be getting longer (more sunshine), and then spring is a mere 90 days after that;-) & I have indoor gardening to do with over-wintered plants). My little circle of life!!====JACK: As the saying goes, "What goes around, comes around." One of my favorite holidays is Feb 2, when I watch the movie, Groundhog Day and wonder what it would be like to be Phil Connors. For me, Feb 2, is the day that announces: .Spring is coming!

FROM PLAIN FOLKS CHESTER: Thanks. I needed that today.====JACK: Thanksgiving is next Thursday. I like that holiday.

FROM SHARIN' SHARON: Three of our church family live in the Brightmoor area. They invited us to a community meeting--requested our support as they made a proposal to those gathered. I didn't know what to expect--so many people have moved out and so many empty houses, etc., but the 45 or so people gathered were so upbeat, some living a long time there, some newer like our three friends, there is a lot of need in that community but with neighborhood people like the ones we met last night, willing to buckle down and support and help all their neighbors to make the community viable long-term--well, it was just very hopeful and sunny. Maybe we'll be able to help somehow too.====JACK: MLK jr gave a speech of hopefulness, saying, "I've been to the mountaintop, and I've seen the Promised Land." Some neighborhoods look pretty dismal, but with upbeat residents, like you describe, the sun will shine again.

FROM BLAZING OAKS: My twin sis and I used to sing "Look For The Silver Lining" (and try to find the sunny side of life!") Now a "golden oldie"! Liked the Longfellow poem, which was new to me. It's been raining for 3 days here in IL after all of our tornadoes (I lost a huge dead tree which took out my electrical lines (and my computer for 3 days...) but now it is cold enough for snow. Going to Chicago for Chicago Chorale Concert this weekend where it will be even colder!!====JACK: That's an optimistic song with music by Jerome Kern and lyrics by Buddy DeSylva. Judy Garland sang a great version of it

FROM JR IN ILLINOIS: I remember a filmstrip I showed in my sixth grade classes about China that quoted a similar proverb: "The mountains can not grow higher, so bit by bit we can make them smaller." ====JACK: I recall something similar in describing eternity. Once every 1000 years a sparrow would come and remove a grain of sand from the mountain. When the mountain was no more, that was the first year of eternity....or something like that.

Thursday, November 21, 2013

Jack's Winning Words 11/21/13

"Seeing is different from being told." (Kenyan Proverb) A Ben Franklin proverb puts it this way. "Tell me, and I forget. Teach me, and I remember. Involve me, and I learn." A friend told me that he learned his "handyman" skills from his father who showed him how to use tools to fix things. Each of us can probably name a skill that we have because someone let us "do" something as a child. My dad played catch with me.   ;-) Jack

FROM RB IN MICHIGAN: These words are so timely for my day.. I not only reflect on my dad, but the many men I observed working in things I love to do today. They involved me in loving others via their God given talents - as you have also done...Thank you,====JACK: We each could make a list of the people who have made us who we are today.

FROM DP IN WISCONSIN: Right-handed or left?====JACK: Ambidextrous! Bert Campaneris played all nine positions in a game on Sept. 8, 1965. His most challenging assignments came in the final two innings. When he took the mound in the eighth he pitched as well as could be expected. On the mound, he pitched ambidextrously, throwing lefty to left-handers, and switched against right-handers. Campy allowed two walks, one hit and one run. Campaneris moved behind the plate in the ninth."

FROM FACEBOOK LIZ: I am an excellent painter (as in house) from helping my dad as a kid. I painted all the muntin bars on his windows.====JACK: I learned how to clean wallpaper and how to remove it. Does anyone do that anymore? BTW, I never knew those window dividers were called muntin bars? vI just knew that I didn't have the patience to paint them.

FROM PEPPERMINT MARY: ....i see..........====JACK: Both sight and insight are great gifts.

FROM HONEST JOHN: I think we learn in various ways and by various means...no need to narrow it down to one way====JACK: The point is...wherever and whenever we learn, learning is best done when the teacher involves us in the process.

FROM SHARIN' SHARON: Actually, think this must really work in handing down an interest in growing plants. You can read a book about it, watch someone else grow them and can sit in a biology class and hear the teacher talk about it but until you get your hands in the soil some and plunk the seed in and then nurture it while it's growing, the experience doesn't seem to get inside and become real until you actually do it. In this regard, people really need the opportunity to make mistakes and see successes and learn--almost like having an original relationship to the plant you're trying to grow. Guess it takes into account that there are a bunch of things that can be different from time-to-time with nature and people.====JACK: I guess that means..When I open my box of Wheaties I should stop and think of what goes into the making of the product. It's like we sing in the hymn: Come, Ye Thankful People, Come..."First the blade and then the ear, Then the full corn shall appear." then the harvester, the miller, the baker, the packager, the grocer.

FROM TAMPA SHIRL: Learn by doing. Unfortunately, I am a bit like Tom Sawyer and will take any help that I can get. All of the electronic stuff these days is quite a challenge.====JACK: My grandson stopped in the other day, and I showed him my new internet modem which needed to be installed. I hadn't gotten around to reading the instructions. let alone getting it to work. He sat at the keyboard and within ten minutes he had everything working just fine.

FROM KF IN MICHIGAN: Cooking, cooking & more cooking. A necessity for feeding 8 people every day!====JACK: Have you passed on your experience by involving your daughters (and husband) in the cooking and cooking in your kitchen?

FROM DOCTOR JUDY: Love this one Jack!! Especially the Ben Franklin proverb.====JACK: Old Ben was really a talented individual...his kite...his glasses...his proverbs...his printing...etc.

FROM BLAZING OAKS: I like Ben's quote, new to me. Margaret Becker at MHS. chose me for student director my Sr. year. She worked with me, so I was able to direct our concert choir in a couple of numbers at the Spring Concert in '48. I'm sure that led me to choose Music Ed. as my college major, and I've directed school and church choirs ever since!   I wrote her a letter to tell her of the influence she'd had in my life. I love getting similar notes from my former students!! We all owe a debt to many "mentors" in our lives!====JACK: Some of my confirmation students receive Winning Words. I enjoy it when one of them will respond by saying, "That's what you taught me in confirmation class."

FROM DP IN MINNESOTA: My Mom was always working on a project like sewing clothing, slip covers, draperies, or knitting or crocheting some useful item. Her practical nature was contagious, and soon I was involved in creating things, with her help of course. I am so grateful for her example because all my life I have enjoyed making things for our children, grandchildren, our homes, and now, especially, making quilts for LWR and the needy in our community.=====JACK: There was a time when mothers were called, "homemakers." When did that go out of style? Here's the 1st verse of a poem that I like...

HOME by Edgar A. Guest

It takes a heap o' livin' in a house t' make it home,

A heap o' sun an' shadder, an' ye sometimes have t' roam

Afore ye really 'preciate the things ye lef' behind,

An' hunger fer 'em somehow, with 'em allus on yer mind.

It don't make any differunce how rich ye get t' be,

How much yer chairs an' tables cost, how great yer luxury;

It ain't home t' ye, though it be the palace of a king,

Until somehow yer soul is sort o' wrapped round everything.

 ====DP: You have a gift of always responding with appropriate thoughts ! Thanks !

 FROM DMF IN MINNESOTA: My dad played catch with me too.....with both arms!====JACK: A few major leaguers could do that, but not many.

 FROM TARMART REV: Running busy and late today, Jack . . . "mentoring" . . . state of the art, highest level of general development!!====JACK: Somebody once said...."I gotta slow down, my feet's movin' too fast!====REV: I remember one time racing my son when he was in Junior

High School, trying to catch him found my head and chest way out in front of my feet to where I had to stop or I would have fallen down . . . my feet couldn't keep up !!

 FROM DB IN MICHIGAN: my grandfather taught me how to drive a nail and to replace the washers on the sink handles in the bathroom, my grandmother taught me how to sew with a needle and thread, my other grandmother taught me how to knit and how to use a sewing machine, an aunt taught me how to crochet ====JACK: My grandmother was in her 90s, and I remember seeing her reading her Bible every day, using a magnifying glass. That impressed me.

Wednesday, November 20, 2013

Jack's Winning Words 11/20/13

"I'm not a genius. I'm just a tremendous bundle of energy." (R. Buckminster Fuller) Futurist (and genius) Bucky Fuller was always a non-conformist. He was expelled from Harvard twice. He had trouble with geometry, and yet was able to invent the geodesic dome   He coined the word, ephemeralization, meaning: to do more with less. Unrelated -- Quarterback Joe Theisman said, "A genius is a guy like Norman Einstein."   ;-) Jack

 FROM MICHIZONA RAY: Genius is currently based on the subjective concepts of what is necessary to test "objectively" and then compare with a standard of "normal" (which is such an impoverished standard for such an evaluation). I would rather use "ephemeralization" as the standard of genius. It is so much more significant!====JACK: I wonder if a measure of "common sense" should be factored into the determination of who is a genius...if common sense can be measured.====RAY: Unfortunately not...because "normal" is as fluid as the sickness of the everyday, and it is determined through the general malaise of the conformed, the politically correct, and the multitude of those who remain asleep (to too much of an extent as critical thinking has seemed to be long past), and this leads to a common sense that has also become something dictated to those who await word as to how and what they are to think and say by those who provide the menu. I particularly love the line, "if you aren't at the table, you're on the menu". That seems to be a good example of common sense.====JACK: Can a test be the judge of "genius"? Or is it the maker of the test? Even Congress can't agree on who should be judges?

 FROM TARMART REV: You are the genius in coming up with some of the most interesting phrases of thought each morning . . . I look for them everyday during the week!! Be blessed, Jack!!====JACK: I like what Aristotle said..."There is no great genius without a mixture of madness."====REV: "The swan glides do smoothly and easily atop the water, while its feet is moving to beat the band underneath to get to its next destination."

 FROM HAWKEYE GEORGE: I think Fuller once conceived a plan to put a dome over St. Louis, back in the 1960s.====JACK: Walt Disney, the master-creator, said: "If you can dream it, you can do it." The optimist is a person who dreams. Or, going back to BCE, Archimedes said, "Give me a lever long enough and a fulcrum on which to place it, and I shall move the world." You learned that in Physics 101, didn't you?

FROM RI IN BOSTON: I had the unique experience of working with Bucky Fuller during my architectural studies at the university. He truly was a phenomenal thinker, and seemed to be inexhaustible when talking about exploring ideas of all sorts. During the period he was working with us at the university, he also gave a couple evening lectures which were open to the public. They attracted a lot of people who had heard about this "genius". After speaking from 8 to 10 p.m. Bucky would suggest a time-out ("Perhaps some of you want to call it an evening") and after a contingent of visitors would leave, Bucky would pick up where he left off, and go on speaking for another hour. The thing is, so much of what he said was fresh thinking, and it captured your attention. BTW, Hawkeye George is correct...In the late '50's Bucky did elaborate about putting a dome over St. Louis, to manage air quality and climate control. A group of architectural students at Washington University, at that time working with Bucky, built a scaled-down dome on the university campus to examine the characteristics of such a structure. St. Louis now has a sizable dome in one of the city parks called the Climatron, a permanent home for a large botanical exhibition.====JACK: You were indeed privileged to be able to be "touched" a couple of geniuses, Bucky and Yama, to name just a couple. Of course, they also had the opportunity "to walk with you," as well.====RI: Both those men were small in stature but giants in creative thinking.=====JACK: I've read that St. Paul was small in stature, too. BTW, how tall do you think that Jesus was?===RI: I've read that Jesus was not tall by today's standards. Unless you are asking about the Jesus who towers over Rio de Janeiro...that's tall.

FROM BBC IN ILLINOIS: Have read a lot of Bucky over the years and heard him speak at Harper College when I was a kid. A most amazing man. They just had a retrospective of his work at the Museum of Contemporary Art . It was wonderful for me to revisit some of his ideas. Had no idea he was expelled twice. That's kind of funny. Another of his words, "Dymaxion" – Dynamic – Maximum – Action (I think) ====JACK: I like manufactured words. Lake Superior State Univ in Michigan makes a list every year of words that should be removed from use and of others that should be added to the dictionary. I wonder if dymaxion is now an approved word.

FROM PLAIN FOLKS CHESTER: Actually, Norman Einstein was Al's older brother, but his folks could not afford college for him. They sent Al instead. Norm went about his business quietly and is not given credit for his many accomplishments. How to make a football hold air was one of them. That's why Theisman remembers him and thinks him a genius. Read the book "Norm and Me." You will be enlightened, as Thomas Edition would say.====JACK: I'm positive that you must be thinking of Norman Vincent, Al Peale's grandson. Dr. Peale would offer prayers for the players before every NY pro football game.

FROM BLAZING OAKS: What a fascinating man! Anyone who is Pres. of Mensa ("74-83) has to be near-genius....His wife of 66 years must have been pretty unflappable!! They died within 36 hours of one another: He had a heart attack while visiting her, when she was dying of cancer in the hospital, and pre-deceased her! Their daughter Allegra was no slouch either, she was "Honoree of the Year" in 1992 of Dance Guild of America, and Prof. of Dance Dep't. of UCLA, and wrote several books about her dad. Allegra's husband, Robert won an Academy Award for his documentary on Micheal Angelo. Seemed to be a brainy bunch on the "Spaceship Earth". I looked up why he was expelled from Harvard :-): 1.) for spending all his money partying with a vaudeville troupe; 2.) for irresponsibility and lack of interest!!   His accomplishments and reputation speak for themselves...I guess he truly "grew up"!====JACK: If my parents were alive, I could explain my grades at Augustana by telling them about Bucky and his grades at Harvard. I'm surprised that one of the TV networks didn't make a show, starring the Fuller family and calling it The Brainy Bunch.

FROM RI: IN BOSTON: The comments from Blazing Oaks regarding the final days of Bucky Fuller and his wife were quite revealing to me. I never heard about the circumstances surrounding their deaths. Reflecting on Bucky's occasional comments while we were privileged to be with him, about his wife's support, I feel certain the two of them were very close. On a couple occasions when he was lecturing publicly, his wife was in the front row, and he identified her to the audience. He joked that the ideal way to theorize and have the means to explore those theories as necessary, was to marry a woman of wealth.

FROM BLAZING OAKS: The Fullers lost their older daughter Alexandra at age four (older than Allegra) due to Meningitis, and Bucky questioned whether it was because of the drafty old house they were living in, in

Chicago, and blamed himself for possibly causing her death. It was a dark time for he and his wife....Allegra named her own daughter Alexandra, after her deceased sister. A lot of times we have no idea what these "public figures" go through.

FROM DB IN MICHIGAN: Buckminsterfullerene: a recently discovered allotrope of carbon, noted for its exquisite shape and design, composed of 60 molecules. The soccer-ball-like structure contains five and six member rings reminiscent of the structure of "geodesic domes" suggested by the late industrial designer Buckminster Fuller. Great name! --kind of like Flash Gordon!====JACK: The more I hear about Fuller, the more impressed I am. Thanks for adding to the lore.

Tuesday, November 19, 2013

Jack's Winning Words 11/19/13

"An optimist figures that taking a step backward after taking a step forward is not a disaster; it's more like the cha-cha." (Sent by Teri Gianetti) Did you know that the NY Yankees have danced the cha-cha to excite their fans? Some good plays could help, too. But that's beside the point. Teri's quote says that the optimist recognizes that life has its setbacks, but when mixed with a positive outlook, we can be dancing. ;-) Jack

FROM RI IN BOSTON: We certainly don't make constant progress in our lives, and not always rapid progress either. We may move forward, then sometimes find that we've lost ground...temporarily, so it's not a "disaster". The WW today reminds me of another comment that goes around, perhaps originating from a realist, "suppose the hokey-pokey is what it's all about!"====JACK: Have you ever danced the Hokey Pokey?====RI: Yes...and done other assorted silly things!====JACK: Have you ever tried to do the "silly walk" as depicted by Monty Python?

FROM HONEST JOHN: Is a typhoon that wipes out most of one's family "a step backward"? More of a cha chaaaaaaaaaa====JACK: As it so often happens, it's the sliver in our finger that gets more attention than what's happening on the other side of the globe to someone unknown to us. That's why there's the need for interpreters. Our Sunday School children took up a collection for the typhoon victims last Sunday.

FROM PEPPERMINT MARY: pollyanna and i very much approve of this outlook on life!====JACK: Why is poor Pollyanna so often depicted in negative terms? Interestingly, it's usually not by children. ====MARY: Are some people of the adult persuasion intimidated by true innocence and optimism? ====JACK: If you have not seen it, you should watch the Twilight Zone episode called, "Kick the Can." Someone commented to me on Sunday, "Isn't it hard to do children's sermons?" I answered, "No! I just try to put myself in the place of the child, and it seems to work out." That's what preaching is about, too.... Trying to put yourself in the pew as well as in the pulpit. That's why you're so good at what you do. You know your audience.====MARY: "kick the can" is a great episode. when working with our children, i feel so close to spirit. just by being together we compose a daily "children's sermon". they are my portal to the other/next world. i am blessed to sit among the audience.

FROM FACEBOOK LIZ: Like.====JACK: Do you "like" dancing the cha-cha, or is it the forward and backward and forward motion of life?====LIZ: i do not dance in public. i do not like the setbacks of life, but who does? i Like the "put it in perspective" of this message.

FROM TARMART REV: "cha-cha" or "square" dancing?? (square: "fair, honest genuine") Remember my old saying? "It was the optimist that invented the airplane, the pessimist that invented the parachute and the realist that flies the plane." ====JACK: I didn't think that the AGs allowed any kind of dancing, unless dancing on the streets of heaven.

FROM CK WHEREVER HE IS: Thanks for the words today Jack! I needed to hear that.====JACK: Did you ever see the commercial for Mennen's Skin Bracer, where a hand comes out and slaps a man across the face, and he responds, "Thanks, I needed that!"? I'm one who likes that product...but not the slap across the face.

FROM PLAIN FOLKS CHESTER: Isn't it true, that n the Cha-cha, while you are moving forward, your partner is moving backward? We need to dance side-by-side. Also,as long as the step forward is longer than the step backward, we are making progress.====JACK: Maybe you can call it the chaaaaa-cha, or the sneeze dance..

FROM TERI GIANETTI: Thanks for printing this & I liked your addition!====JACK: I got a lot of good feedback on that quote. Thanks for sending it. ====TERI: By the way, anyone that knows how to really cha-cha, knows there are cooperative "side moves" and no one ever takes all the steps back. Interesting interpretations. And, by the way, the cha cha one was not my favorite quote. My favorite ones are: "Even a piece of paper has two sides." "Change is the only constant." My most favorite quote is: "Out beyond ideas of right thinking and wrong thinking, there is a field. I'll meet you there." (Rumi) Responses would probably be really interested!

 FROM SBP IN FLORIDA: I'm either a pragmatist or a fool....or some of both. Setbacks provide breathing time...reflection time...planning the next step time.... That sounds "holier than thou"....but it's in the same league (I think,) as "God doesn't shut a door without opening a window."....my way of keeping mental balance.====JACK: Every day is decision-making time. I like the Ella Fitzgerald song, "Undecided." "First, you say, you do And then you don't And then you say, you will And then you won't You're undecided now So what are you gonna do?" Even sitting on the fence is a decision. I like your suggestion to use "down" time as "reflection" time.

Monday, November 18, 2013

Jack's Winning Words 11/18/13

"I have more zits now than I had as a teenager--stress zits!" (Tiffani Thiessen) Have you ever heard of stress zits? Studies have shown that stress and acne can be related. Psychologist Lisa Klewicki (3 Minutes a Day) suggests 3 ways to handle stress. 1) Look for the positives. 2) Set and follow priorities. 3) Practice gratitude. If you're concerned about stress and how you look, follow Dr. K's suggestions...starting today. ;-) Jack

FROM TARMART REV: ... or you could walk around West Bloomfield singing, "Think Positive" from Willy Wonka!!====JACK: I don't know that song, but maybe Target and Walmart will let you sing it to the customers as they do their Christmas shopping on Black Friday. Google tells me that the song starts out...

You've nothing to lose, so why not choose to think positive?

Whenever my luck is on the blink I think positive.

Whenever I'm feeling down and out and don't know what to do,

I never give way to fear and doubt 'cause thinking positive sees me through

FROM WATERFORD JAN: I'm not worried about my zits. When I was 17 my doctor told me I would outgrow them. I'm 78 and I'm still waiting, but I'm not worried!====JACK: For some people...It's once a kid, always a kid.

Friday, November 15, 2013

Jack's Winning Words 11/15/13

"There is no more lovely and charming relationship than a good marriage." (Martin Luther) Luther said that he found peace when he married Katherine. Did you know that he helped her escape from a nunnery in a fish barrel? Theirs was a lively and a happy home. Most people have some "lively" stories to tell about the home in which they were raised. Maybe some were charming, depending on who's telling the story.   ;-) Jack

FROM TARMART REV: I'm sure many more stories are about to be created in this next month and one-half!! Happy Holidays forthcoming!!====JACK: Stories are created every day. My sister-in-law said to a friend, "Your husband must be a barrel of laughs." The wife replied, "Yeah..." You can add the nuance.

FROM SHARIN' SHARON: I was raised in a lively home. One of my most precious memories is when the old farm house burned down, somehow Dad rented another farm house, people were giving us furniture, etc., and that first night us kids were sleeping on mattresses in one bedroom, mom and dad were on a mattress in their bedroom and they just started laughing and laughing because dad's cowboy boots beside the mattress were sticking up so high. They showed me what character and endurance and fortitude and faith and love were all about. But they weren't always happy and showed me how to get through those times too. ====JACK: I was unsuccessful in finding the exact quote...but it has to do with staying calm when everything around you is burning. Were you in the farmhouse when it started to burn? Fire can be devastating.

FROM HAWKEYE GEORGE: You're spot-on!====JACK: A couple of older people that I know use the term, spot-on. I know what it implies, but I'll have to look up the derivation. (I looked it up) Answer:
The phrase 'spot on', meaning 'in exactly the right place, comes to us from India and the snooker-based game of billiards. The six coloured balls were each placed on their respective 'spots' on the table after having been sunk. The placement of these coloured balls, unlike the red balls, which were permanently 'sunk' when potted, was critical to the

game, so the person re-spotting the coloured balls (other than red, of course) would have to be precisely on the correct spot, or, 'spot on' for the game to be fairly played. The critical nature originated from the size of the table; 6' x 12', and the tightness of the pockets; 1.5 x ball diameter, unlike today's 'sloppy' 2 x ball diameter

FROM RI IN BOSTON: The liveliness at home while I grew up came from doing what was necessary to put food on the table, clothes on the kids, and pay the rent. The depression years were tough, so my father took jobs of yard cleaning and gardening, and my mother did laundry and ironing for college students in our town. It wasn't actually "lovely and charming" as they sacrificed to stay afloat, but they never quarreled about it nor gave any indication of how dire things were. They prevailed with faith, and by the grace of God the latter years of their 66 years in marriage turned into years of plenty. My regret is that I didn't do enough to express my thanks to them for the many hardships they had endured over the years.====JACK: As the saying goes, "We are who we were." We need to keep that in mind as we examine our life and the life of those around us. I don't think that any of us have said "thank you" enough to those who have shaped our life.

FROM CZB: I think I know why you picked this one today!====JACK: You noticed?

FROM JR IN CALIFORNIA: HOW TRUE!====JACK: There are times when we recognize this truth more deeply.

FROM PLAIN FOLKS CHESTER: My parents thoroughly enjoyed each other and it rubbed of on us. Don't be afraid to disagree sometimes. Makes for a more lively, loving marriage.====JACK: To disagree, but not in a disagreeable way.====PFC: Amen! During our premarital conference with Dean Johnson, he advised us not to use the phrase "You always..." and we never forgot it. He was a neat guy.

FROM DC IN KANSAS: I recall some reports about Luther's choice of Katie. Did I learn it at the Sem? Luther assisted the nuns "escape," and Luther found partners for all except Katie. So he stepped up to the challenge.====JACK: I remember reading that Luther said to her: "I'm old enough to be your father." I can't remember the context...but it was probably part of a lively discussion between the two of them.

FROM OUTHOUSE JUDY: Ours is certainly a happy loving family. We are deeply grateful for each other and the spouses God has given each of us. We stick together during the "crisis times" and the ill times and the happy times. For this we are most grateful.====JACK: Is it charming, too?

FROM BLAZING OAKS: Spot on indeed! Bill and I were very different in many ways, but as his mother used to say, "If two people think exactly alike, one of them is not needed!" :-) Together we made a good team in ministry. I remember (brother-in-law) Hal telling of Luther "freeing" the nuns!   Yes, a good marriage is such a blessing!!!====JACK: I'm sure that your children remember a "lively" household. Charming?

Thursday, November 14, 2013

Jack's Winning Words 11/14/13

"Let me be a little kinder, Let me be a little blinder, To the faults of those around me." (Edgar A. Guest) EAG was a columnist for the Detroit Free Press and his job was to come up with a poem for every issue. Most of them were homespun thoughts, not considered great poetry in the academic sense. Maybe that's why so many people liked them. We need to be reminded that kindness would make this a better world. ;-) Jack

FROM HONEST JOHN: guest is recommending stupidity. I think kindness is being aware of your neighbor's faults but not reminding him of them every second====JACK: I see that you've decided not to take Edgar's advice.

FROM PEPPERMINT MARY: I have a car magnet that says, "kindness matters". whenever anyone comments on it I give it to them to display on their car. I bought several for back-ups. I'm hoping it will turn into a movement! (me and arlo!)====JACK: You gave me one of those magnets. No one has commented on it...yet, but seeing it on the trunk lid has motivated me to do some "little" acts of kindness. Thanks!

FROM TARMART REV: Brought back a memory of Will Rogers from Oklahoma for some reason . . . probably for him being noted for his colloquialism! I'm going out today, taking your advice . . . spreading a little kindness!!====JACK: Just for fun...Keep track of the times today that people show kindness to you. Will one outperform the other?====REV: Will do my best to do so and report back tomorrow. 0;-) PS...Interesting day yesterday as I spoke to a ladies' class of 20 or so at the local Evangelical Free Church about my experiences in reaching out to the community, especially with Wal-Mart and Target in mind. They were just finishing up a series of lessons on witnessing and wanted to look at ways they could put their desire to do so to work for them. Someone had mentioned my name as one to speak to them about it. -- Last evening it was sharing on AA's topic, "Spirituality" with an addiction group at our Woodland Centers that deal with addictions. Usually once or twice a year I'm asked to share. Quite a diversity of expression given yesterday.

FROM GOOD DEBT JON: I like this. Reminds me of Samuel Johnson's words, "While fondness may not always be within our abilities, kindness is always possible. " (I paraphrase from memory)====JACK: Acts of kindness will become a "memory" reaction, if we do them often enough.

FROM MICHIZONA RAY: I think maybe when Jesus said that the poor will always be with you, He might have also said that the unkind, the mean-spirited, the self-righteous, the destructive, the manipulators, etc., will always be with us as well. We can't "change" others, and lines are seemingly drawn that make even influencing others less frequent. So, we can certainly endure to be kind amidst those who choose otherwise. ====JACK: Jesus probably didn't say that the mean-spirited and self-righteous will always be with us, because he was a positive thinker who could foresee the possibility of redemption in everyone.====RAY: Proverbs notes how "arguments" with the foolish is foolishness by the one arguing. I'm not sure positive thinking means being blind to foolishness, but loving the fool -- not for one's choice of foolishness (if one did choose it), but for the wisdom to choose Love instead. Jesus also knows that there are those who will reject or have rejected Him. I don't think He loves them any less; but I think He will let them go their way just the same. After all, we ate from the tree of the Knowledge of Good and Evil even though we were told we "shall certainly die"... And God didn't stop us! Instead, He loved us enough to send His Son. Many are called; but not all answer wisely. And I can still be positive.====JACK: All I'm saying is that I believe God never writes anyone off so long as there is sand left in the hour glass.====RAY: Amen...and I am saying the same. Being kind amidst "reason" to otherwise assumes the sand has run out. So, being kind to the one whose sand has run through the hourglass would be all the more Christian!

 FROM SHARIN' SHARON: I'm very sensitive to criticism and aware of having so many things wrong with me but always pray to really soak it up that I am forgiven and that it is God who is constantly helping me, through so many others, with this miserable condition and terrible weakness because, at the same time, have become aware that people who are really hard and demanding and critical of themselves have a tendency to lay such heavy burdens on others around them too. Don't want to be blinder, just want to keep on knowing God in myself and others better. Thanks for your WW words today--thought-provoking once again. You never let us down in provoking us to cogitate.====JACK: Jesus said, "Come unto me, all ye who labor and are heavy laden and sensitive to criticism, and I will give you rest." Take your burden to the Lord and LEAVE it there.

FROM IKE AT THE MIC: On that theme: I 'm reminded of advice for a good marriage:"Before you get married you should go in with your eyes wide open, once you're married you should spend the rest of your relationship with your eyes 1/2 closed"..====JACK: ...and all this time I thought you were squinting because of the bright lights in the TV studio.

FROM TAMPA SHIRL: That is definitely what the whole world needs-more kindness. Les has that book in his collection. You are very kind to pass along your winning words every day.====JACK: A favorite of mine is the Bacharach/David song, "What the Word Needs Now Is Love, Sweet Love," I think I'll Google YouTube and listen to Dionne Warwick sing it...Now!

FROM WATERFORD JAN: No one ever had to have anyone explain the meaning of Edgar A. "Bud" Guest's poetry. They struck a chord in the same way that Winning Words do.====JACK: I can understand and appreciate that there are nuances to great poetry, but I usually like stuff that rhymes. I also like the common poetic writings of Carl Sandburg.

FROM BLAZING OAKS: As I indicated earlier, I feel Kindness is one of the most important attributes in a spouse. Certainly makes him/her "wear well" over the years!! I like the Samuel Johnson quote in your blog (Good Debt Jon). So true; We can't "LOVE" everyone, but we can be kind! "God is within: Don't be without!' (David Shouldice)====JACK: People have had a lot to say about kindness. Being blind to some of the things that "irk" us can be a good attribute, as well...remembering that we're not always right.

Wednesday, November 13, 2013

Jack's Winning Words 11/13/13

"God delights in concealing things; scientists delight in discovering things." (New reading of Proverbs 25:2) In seminary biblical studies I learned these words regarding the Old and New Testaments..."The New is in the Old concealed; the Old is in the New revealed." In other words, God has a way of showing himself in both the Old and the New. Did it ever occur to you that God might like to play, Hide and Seek?   ;-) Jack

 FROM RB IN MICHIGAN: Ah ha! This is why there is "Gospel" in both the Old and New Testaments...
Always enjoy your take on life via winning words. What does the "c" stand for? Is there a little christian (c) waiting to come out in all.====JACK: There's "Law" in both, too. If Gospel means, good news, does Law mean, bad news? BTW, the "c" is part of a secret code to determine where my customers are.====RB: I agree there is law in both, but many will say NT is all Gospel. The contrary of this like many statements is false. This is why the high priests, scribes, and Sadducees had such a hard time understanding Christ (our big C) - no code required :) By the way didn't you teach me that all we come in contact with are c's = community? God's blessings on your day.====JACK: I've learned that

it is a never ending quest to bring harmony among all who have their way of interpreting the Bible, or religion in general.

FROM MICHIZONA RAY: I have often wondered "why" about many things like life-on-earth, suffering, temporal V. Eternity, spatial V. Infinity, Grace and not Grace, temptation, and many more! I know I may never know or understand them; but I wonder about them just the same. Do you suppose God giggles at even our contemplations for that which is hidden and exposed?====JACK: My mother used to do embroidery. Her work was beautiful, until you looked at the underside. That was a mess. Could it be that God is an embroiderer, too, and when we see life as a "mess," we're simply looking at the underside of God's work?

FROM TARMART REV: "In the fullness of time . . . " My mind this morning was taken back because of your posting to the chronological order of years and historical moments highlighted at the new Holocaust Center in Farmington Hills. I would enjoy studying that once again . . . maybe next year.====JACK: We continue to search for the hidden "good" in the Holocaust event.====REV: Yes we do . . . emotionally moved each time I visit the memorial . . . worshipping at Temple Kol Ami those five years and having somewhat of a relationship with Rabbi Conrad will always be a highlight in my life.====JACK: A Christian congregation worshipping in a Jewish Temple certainly made a statement in our community. It's too bad that it wasn't able to continue...but life goes on. Only G-d is forever.

FROM FACEBOOK LIZ: Interesting. With the recent discovery of 8 billion other "earths," it seems God has more to reveal & we, to discover...====JACK: One of the lessons taught by diversity is that there are others in the world (universe) besides us. I try hard to look at others and see them as individuals, like myself.

 FROM JT IN MICHIGAN: No, I never thought of God playing hide and seek, but with Scripture study I am finally seeing how everything in the Old Testament is preparation for the New. Am studying Revelation this year and unwrapping the symbolism John uses. (I wonder if he ever thought he'd be writing for such a lightweight as me?)====JACK: Jesus seemed to identify more with the "lightweights" of society than with those who had all of the answers. Karl Barth, the famous theologian, was asked to explain his belief in God. He responded, "Jesus loves me, this I know, for the Bible tells me so." Don't become too worked up about the Book of Revelation. Even those who determined which books should be in the Bible struggled over its inclusion. It squeaked in.

FROM BLAZING OAKS: I LIKE THE SEMINARY SAYING ABOUT OLD AND NEW....IT'S AS GOOD AS "YOU CAN'T UNSCREW THE INSCRUTABLE" THAT YOU QUOTED ONCE, AND I ALWAYS REMEMBERED! NEAT TURN OF PHRASE.   WHEN YOU REALIZE THAT ALL THAT EXISTS FROM ANY ORIGINAL MANUSCRIPT OF THE NEW TESTAMENT IS A SCRAP OF PAPYRUS NO BIGGER THAN A CREDIT CARD, WITH A COUPLE OF VERSES FROM THE GOSPEL OF JOHN, AND ALL THE REST ARE COPIES OF COPIES OF COPIES (HAND DONE IN THE EARLY CENTURIES!)...YOU DO REASON THAT TO KNOW THE WHOLE TRUTH AND NOTHING BUT THE TRUTH, WILL HAVE TO WAIT UNTIL "WE KNOW, EVEN AS WE'RE

KNOWN" IN THE NEXT PHASE OF ETERNAL LIFE !====JACK: There's a lot that is contained in that small word, faith. Mark Twain tried to be humorous when he said, "Faith is believing what you know ain't so." But, when you've had to lean on it, faith ain't so funny.

 FROM SHARIN' SHARON: Actually, it was in a church Bible study with Pastor Schulz, studying in the group the book of Isaiah, that I had a deep faith experience so that started trusting more and more in scripture, growing faith in God and believing that His church carries His Word for us. Ever since then, I've believe that God can come to anyone He chooses as they are reading and studying any part of the Bible He chooses to talk to us through. It's all pertinent to someone's faith journey and when once you find one scripture passage meaningful, seems to me a person starts wondering and looking to see if any other scripture passage says something personal to oneself too. Does God hide himself and keep secrets--I don't believe so, it is our condition that makes us thus so in the relationship. The wonder and miracle to me is that the scientists keep on looking.====JACK: There's nothing wrong with a God who enjoys playfulness. In school I recall how satisfying it was to come up with a right answer after studying and studying. ====SHARON: Thinking some more about this and actually, I believe God can come to us however we, in our sinful nature, open ourselves up to receiving Him. There must be something God puts in us that makes us all keep at it, since He created us maybe he put questions we have the audacity to think we originated ourselves in us too. Wouldn't that be humorous? Or do we need to think we can think so much ourselves? What makes God delight in us? What makes us delight in God?

Tuesday, November 12, 2013

Jack's Winning Words 11/12/13

"Nothing is a waste of time if you use the experience wisely."
(Auguste Rodin) Rodin lived these words of his. Even though the realism of his sculptures was criticized by the art world of his day, he refused to change his style. Recently, a casting of The Thinker sold for $15+M. At a Rodin showing in Detroit, I learned that The Thinker is part of a larger sculpture, where he's looking down upon people in Hell...and thinking.
;-) Jack

 FROM BLAZING OAKS: It seems that a quote from baseball player Ichiro Suzuki is appropriate here:"People striving for approval from others become phony." It is sad that so many talented artists have not been appreciated in their lifetimes, nor reaped the financial benefits of their talents; However they remain true to themselves, for their Art's sake! It boggles my mind that that amount of money is paid for art work (or anything else!). I always think of all the good it could do for hungry and disadvantaged people!! But as my husband used to say, "It's not what you'd do with a million, if fortune should be your lot; It's what you're doing now with the buck and a half you've got!"=====JACK: As with the story of the Widow's Mite...It's not how much you have that's important, but what you do with what you have. Or, when the woman washed Jesus' feet with expensive ointment. The complaint was that this ointment could have been sold and the money used for better things, like helping the poor.

FROM TARMART REV: Could we agree that "that is a Hell of a sculpture in downtown Detroit?" I always wondered what was behind that . . . thank you, Jack, for enlightening me this early morning!!====JACK: Today is Rodin's birthday. His gift to the world of The Thinker has given us something to think about.

FROM PH IN MINNESOTA: is it also true that he was sitting on a toilet??====JACK: As people age, they tend to think about things like trips to the bathroom.====PH: my Dad, in his old age, used to say that he spent 1/3 of his time sleeping, 1/3 trying to remember someone's name, and 1/3 of his time looking for the men's room... this is not nearly as funny as it used to be!====JACK: I used to think that my dad was old, but now I have become older than he was at the time. Now, I think that Methuselah (969) was old.

FROM PLAIN FOLKS CHESTER: If you can't play the mandolin, don't criticize the one who can. ====JACK: There's a mandolin song called, "Losing My Religion," but I'd be afraid to play it.====PFC: Do you play the mandolin? I took piano lessons when I turned 60 so I am a critic.====JACK: If you live long enough you might be able to play the piano like Phil Connors in the movie, Groundhog Day..

FROM ML IN MICHIGAN: A friend of mine sent me this quote, though I don't know the author.
"Wherever creative love enriches life, the Holy Spirit is present and operating." She suggested I use it as a lens for certain things that are bothering me. I like it. Of course, I suppose, the trick is to recognize

creative love.====JACK: The Holy Spirit works in some mysterious ways which are beyond our understanding. Hardly a day goes by, except that I recognize the Holy Spirit affecting my life. And the Holy Spirit is affecting things, whether or not I recognize it...too. When things bother us, it's good to remember that the Holy Spirit is always at work.

 FROM TAMPA SHIRL: How true that is. When we visited his studio and museum and garden, several years ago, the entire area was conducive to thinking and enjoying.====JACK: I wonder how many "snubbed" artists of today will gain recognition with the passage of time? Happy Birthday, Rodin!

Monday, November 11, 2013

Jack's Winning Words 11/11/13

"There's not a day goes by when I don't get up and say thank you to somebody." (Rod Stewart) On this Veterans Day I say Thank You to a friend who never made it back alive from Viet Nam. It's good when we can thank people in person for what they have done for us...parents, friends, the unknowns. Nov. 11 has been designated as a time to show appreciation for those who have given part, if not all, of their life, to help preserve the American way of life. Words seem hardly adequate. "Thank you!"   ;-) Jack

 FROM HY YO SILVER: Thanks for YOUR service, Jack.====JACK: Some "serve" by standing on the curb and cheering as the heroes pass by. I'm a curbside flag waver.

FROM TARMART REV: I add my "Thank you!" as well. "Thank you!"====JACK: Up there is Scandinavian country, you should say, "tack så mycket!"====REV: I'm sure I must agree!! In our Assembly when someone speaks forth like this, we always await the interpretation so the whole body might be edified.
====JACK: In the ELCA, we Google.

FROM SHARIN' SHARON: The military men/women whom I've known who came back from wars have been so changed. Living life before and after a war experience, at least from what I see, changes us in the U.S.A. too. It's not just a "job", it really is sacrificial and ultimately all of us who didn't go have to deal with this sacrificial aspect of protecting our country's freedom. It's true, words are hardly adequate but still we try with "thank you."====JACK: I personally know of a WW 2 veteran who was a medic and had to treat the wounded and dying as they were brought home on a hospital ship. He never would talk about it. "You don't want to know." He wanted no parades, no honor. General Sherman gave his "War is Hell" speech just a few miles from where I now live. Of course, this does not preclude us from saying, Thank You!

FROM THE CHRISTOPHERS' (3 MINUTES A DAY): On his farm, Doug Schmidgall created a unique display of appreciation for military veterans. Using a 20-foot-wide disc that he attached to the back of his tractor, he carved out the heartwarming words "Thank You Troops" on a hill near the Abraham Lincoln Capital Airport serving Springfield, Illinois.

According to Illinois' State Journal-Register, the farmer's grateful message stretched across a hill about seven football fields wide and 100 yards tall. Schmigdall, who has two sons in the military, says that whenever he sees a veteran he makes a point to shake his or her hand and say thank you. "They all deserve it," he affirmed.

FROM FACEBOOK LIZ: You said it well...Thank you to all veterans & their families.====JACK: I know that some fly the flag every day. I put ours out on special occasions, like today.

FROM BADGER DONNA: Love this and THANKS Jack.====JACK: One of the soldiers who raised the flag on Mt. Suribachi (Iwo Jima) was from Antigo, Wisconsin.

FROM RI IN BOSTON: Passing out thank-yous is a simple gesture that can mean a lot to those you give the favor. It takes very little effort, and (going back to last week's WW) like Bear Bryant said, "It don't cost nuthin'!" Regarding our veterans as we do on this day of special recognition for them, we can't say too much in appreciation for their service. They have given greatly "to help preserve the American way of life", though I'm not convinced the American way of life we are witnessing these days is the same American way of life of the past, that most of us still hang on to.====JACK: As the saying goes, "Beauty is in the eye of the beholder." Thus, the "American Way of life" is in the eye of the beholder. Each generation has its pluses and minuses. I tend to accentuate the positive and eliminate the negative.

FROM BLAZING OAKS: MY BILL, WHO WAS A NAVY VETERAN OF WW 2, OFTEN TALKED OF CLASSMATES AND GUYS HE SERVED WITH WHO NEVER MADE IT BACK HOME TO MARRY, RAISE A FAMILY, HAVE A PROFESSIONAL LIFE, AND RUED THE WASTE OF IT ALL. MY DEAR FRIEND LOST HER HANDSOME HUSBAND IN THE PHILIPPINES, WHILE THE MOTHER OF TWO SMALL BOYS, AND EXPECTING THEIR THIRD ...IN WW2. SHE NEVER REMARRIED, AND RAISED HER FAMILY ALONE.(DID A GOOD JOB!) AND WAS A SCRATCH GOLFER, AND ACTIVE CHURCH AND SCHOOL WORKER. SHE'S 89 NOW, AND STILL MOURNS WHAT THEY ALL LOST WHEN HIS PLANE WENT DOWN. BRINGS IT HOME FOR ME..====JACK: There are many "what if" stories that come out of war and of tragedy, but we move on. The believer knows that Good Friday was followed by Easter..

FROM OUTHOUSE JUDY: Gary's nephew is in Special Ops, my brother-in-law is in the Army in Grayling and our son-in-law is a Vet. We are thankful for all of the men and women who have kept us free. God bless them all! ====JACK: I wonder if there's a different feeling between those who were "drafted" and those who "enlisted?" All you served are veterans. I remember how parents and spouses proudly displayed in their front window a star (blue or gold) for each loved one who was in the military. ====JUDY: We owned a big field in Harper Woods with a county ditch running along the edge on the other side. The field is still known today as "Chappel Field". The field was a major hangout for all the guys in our neighborhood because it was big enough for a baseball field. Needless to say, it was filled with our friends from school. We played baseball nearly everyday. Those boys were welcomed into our family by my parents and we would have a big picnic all the time. Well, most of those boys were drafted and some enlisted. Of those boys, three didn't come back from Vietnam. It was heartbreaking. But you couldn't tell who was drafted and who enlisted, because they were all proud to serve. I think the parents were more upset about the drafted boys though. We still remember them all.

Friday, November 08, 2013

Jack's Winning Words 11/8/13

"Lord, prop us up on our leanin' side." (An old man's prayer) A friend of mine used to enjoy taking pictures of old barns. Some were "leaning" like in the old man's prayer. With the passing of time, we, like the old barn, often need some propping up. In fact, it's not always a matter of age. Where do you go when you're leanin'? I guess it's different for each of us. What are your props? Prayer is a help for me. So are friends.   ;-) Jack

 FROM MICHIZONA RAY: For me, it's trusting that people (in general) will respond with integrity (which would include a whole page to explicate). I require a lot of "leaning" on Hope in those circumstances. I trust my Faith in God's guiding hand, hoping man will not reject it. Over the years, I have become more convinced that innocence (not ignorance) is bliss. And, once one's innocence is lost, one cannot go back into the Garden of Eden where bliss reigned supreme. Ignorance is more like pretending that one is innocent of the mess that is all around him/her. (The Christian Pollyanna comes to mind.) This doesn't mean I don't like people; because people are one of my favorite blessings in life. But, I have developed a trust in our weaknesses and our vanity instead of the innocence that hopes for continuous righteousness and perfection. It's not a negative viewpoint; just an honest one that accepts our limitations. Hence, I must lean! I think it is in Psalm 84, last verse, "blessed are those who trust in the Lord". ====JACK: That Psalm verse could be translated, "Blessed are those who lean on the Lord." Besides that, a prop for me are the responses (like yours) that I get from those who read Winning Words.

FROM PH IN MINNESOTA: i wouldn't say that i was leanin' at the time but you were certainly a kind of prop for me when i first began my ministry, as was L.T., and a number of others. its good to think back over our lives as remember those who helped us along the way.====JACK: We may not be aware of it...but we're always leanin' and in danger of falling on our face, except for our friends and the grace of God..

FROM SHARIN' SHARON: Prayer is definitely a help for me. Plus also strongly believing that God answers prayer. When my own congregation seemed not to be transparent (in my eyes), and I felt lonely about the inclusion of openly GLBT people in the Church, God opened the way for me to become a participant of All God's Children in the nearby, within walking distance, Presbyterian Church group where all the people are very comfortable with inclusion and openness. When my own congregation was in the throes of calling a new Pastor and again things were fairly crazy and not open, God opened the way for me to have the sacramental oil of the healing mass in the Catholic Church, again within walking distance. when a person is wisest to keep quiet, to keep the peace and wait on God to work among us, it is my belief that God gives us a place (guess it's the barn behind the house) and people to lean on and, while keeping on hoping and caring and loving, it's awesome to start being a part of what God does do then in the house. Amen ====JACK: I've learned not to give up on God. His time and his ways are not always in sync with ours.

 FROM MOLINER MAR: My "prop" is a walk in the woods behind my house. A bench out there is a great place to sit and "meditate", or just to sit and let the beauty of the day prop me up. Old barns are a treasure and take us back to the gentler times of our lives. (I spent my early years on a farm, so seeing barns props me up.)====JACK: When I was a kid in Moline, we used to have a "fort" built in the side of a hill in Morgan Park where we'd go to plan our next adventure. All age groups need their props.

 FROM RI IN BOSTON: My three year old granddaughter is my mainstay. She's able to encourage new vitality from this old body of mine. It seems Isaiah 11:6 got it right..."a little child shall lead them." ====JACK: Wouldn't it be a boring life if the generations didn't come and go? It's sad to say, "Good-bye," but it's refreshing to say, "Hello!"====RI: Everything around us seems to emulate Nature...constantly renewing itself...whether we like it or not. I agree it's refreshing to say "Hello" and allow new things a chance.====JACK: The good-byes are not always so easy.

FROM OUTHOUSE JUDY: I do my leanin' on the Lord. He's always there for us. He's the Rock we use.   (Sorry I have not written back in awhile.) I am fighting the good fight of several immune disorders. And lastly, my 20 year old cousin was in a car accident and was air-lifted to U of M Hospital where he is on life support.====JACK: The Lord also uses us to help prop others. The prop-ee can become the prop-er.

FROM IKE AT THE MIC: On this theme,I thought you might want to know that that the Leaning Tower of Pisa was purchased by the Hilton Hotel Chain & their plans are to call it the "TILTEN HILTON" ====JACK: It sounds as though you've been tiltin' a few too many.

FROM TARMART REV: In constant conversation and thought with my Creator, friends, inspiring sermons and Bible studies dealing with my area of concern . . . history has proven, my weakest link is sitting all the while reading a lengthy book (shorter articles catch my attention much better).====JACK: Have your sermons grown progressively shorter in order to capture the listener who have an attention span like yours?

FROM PLAIN FOLKS CHESTER: Don't use a prop as a crutch. The "list" can become permanent. ====JACK: I've never seen a barn on crutches.====PFC: next time you take me so literally, I am going to assign you to my SPAM box

FROM DFL IN OREGON: "Winning Words" is a large prop also! Thanks, Jack.====JACK: I hear that, occasionally, and it makes the 5 am time at the computer worthwhile for me.

Tuesday, December 31, 2013

Jack's Winning Words 1/31/13

"All you take with you is that which you've given away." (Inscription under Peter Bailey's picture) Peppermint Mary noticed these words while watching the classic film, "It's A Wonderful Life." Recently my daughters saw that movie and got to meet ZuZu afterward. George Bailey must have taken after his father, because he was always trying to help people. The world is a better place, because of people like George. ;-) Jack

FROM TARMART REV: Had the privilege of being a bearer of good tidings again this Christmas season...two separate sources contributed, one $650.00 and the other, $2000.00...unfortunately to some extend, because of the busyness of the church activities in the two weeks before Christmas, I didn't come across the $2000.00 Christmas card until Christmas Day when I finally took time to open our cards and reflect upon them...I had thought the gentleman in Minneapolis perhaps didn't send his card this year...I was looking for it, but had not seen it come through and surprisingly found he had doubled the amount this year...so--- started late, but half way through now distributing his gifts to surprised, but very appreciative folk this Christmas season....... . . here was the distribution for the $650.00.

Good afternoon to my special friends of the Barney Family . . . Please find below a report indicating the gifts of money distributed to some very surprised and grateful folk this Christmas season. Thank you once again for allowing me the privilege of being the bearer of good tidings to some less fortunate people and families this Christmas season. HPMc

$150 Single mother fighting eating disorder, in clinic and needing housing for a week...placed in motel for a week...(Sara)

$50 Mother/Daughter Christmas meal while visiting invalid father in Olivia Nursing Home (Denise)

$50 Recent needy widow...first Christmas without husband (Rita)

$50 Special needs' gentleman living in downtown (Frieda's Cafe)

$100 Single mother of two grade school girls...father not paying child support as he should (Armanda)

$50 Single mother walking through a broken relationship at Christmastime (Leah)

$50 Down and outer with gas money (Keith)

$50 Widow with two boys at home (Lucina)

$50 Homeless man sleeping in his car needing money to help pay for motel for a month. (Brian)

$50 Man walking the streets...gave him money for a Christmas meal. (Mike)

====JACK: It's a wonderful life, isn't it, when you are able to give help to people in need?

FROM MICHIZONA RAY: This is so true. It seems that the seeds of righteousness bear fruits that return in multiples, and when given away, foster a fuller, richer inner vineyard. ...Just that much more to give away! So I suppose maybe you do take it with you!====JACK: I've commented before about the saying attached to my computer..."Anyone can count the seeds in an apple, but only God can count the apples in a seed."

FROM PEPPERMINT MARY: i feel a little bit wise and honored. happy new year to you all! ====JACK: It just proves that I read and appreciate your responses. HNY backatcha.

 FROM MW IN ILLINOIS: This is one of my favorite movies, always watch at least once during the season.====JACK: You're not the only one who likes it. It's considered to be one the 100 best movies ever made.

 FROM RS IN TEXAS: You are so right, Jack. Being from Michigan you probably have seen this, but just in case...........http://www.youtube.com/v/0Ejh_hb15Fc?version=3&hl=en_US&rel=0...====JACK: No, I had not see that TV clip, but I do know of Olivet, Michigan, and I was moved by the action of their football team...and the tear on the cheek of one of their players.

 FROM TRIHARDER: "And in the end, the love you take is equal to the love you make." Lennon/McCartney (from Abbey Road)

 FROM BM IN MICHIGAN: Thanks for giving me something to think about almost every day.

 FROM GOOD DEBT JON: Sadder than leaving it, all are folks that allow their possessions to "own" them while they are here. Happy New Year to all. We are preparing for the best year ever, I hope I can live up to the opportunities in front of me.

FROM HAWKEYE GEORGE: Just about my favorite movie - we usually watch it every year.

FROM BLAZING OAKS: WISE WORDS AND HOW ASTUTE OF PEPPERMINT MARY TO NOTICE THAT! IT IS OUR TURN TO FEED THE HOMELESS TONIGHT, ON NEW YEAR'S EVE, (AND VERY COLD!) WE'RE PREPARING FOR OVER A HUNDRED. HOT CHILI, CHILI-DOGS, FRUIT, DRINKS CHIPS, AND DESSERT; AFTER WHICH I'LL JOIN FRIENDS AT FIRST NIGHT IN SPRINGFIELD TO RING IN A NEW YEAR, AND ANOTHER CHANCE TO "MAKE A DIFFERENCE"! WE ARE SO BLESSED!!

FROM SHARIN' SHARON: "Life of the Beloved" by Henri Nouwen, page 124 "You and I would dance for joy were we to know truly that we, little people, are chosen, blessed, and broken to become the bread that will multiply itself in the giving. You and I would no longer fear death, but live toward it as the culmination of our desire to make all of ourselves a gift for others. The fact that we are so far from that state of mind and heart shows only that we are mere beginners in the spiritual life and have not yet fully claimed the full truth of our call. But let us be thankful for every little glimpse of the truth that we can recognize and trust that there is always more to see--always."

FROM OUTHOUSE JUDY: Neither Gary or I have ever seen the movie but I hear it's good. The inscription is wonderful though and we all know it's true. Have a blessed New Year. We are spending it with our little granddaughters and tomorrow will be another big family day! That's the best way to start off the new year! ====JACK: You've never seen that movie? There's even an angel in it.

Monday, December 30, 2013

Jack's Winning Words 12/30/13

"Something good eventually emerges from something bad. As a consequence, weaknesses often become strengths." (Australian Wisdom) At age 6, Pete Gray lost his arm in a accident. Despite his adversity, and with determination, he became a major league baseball player. In one of his letters, St. Paul wrote: "By the grace of God, when I am weak, then I am strong." Have you experienced good coming from bad?   ;-) Jack

 FROM HAWKEYE GEORGE: Many, many times.==JACK: Every athlete knows the truth of this quote..."You win some, you lose some. But you live to fight another day."==GEORGE: I'd also include small business owners, too.

 FROM MICHIZONA RAY: A farmer's perspective of manure brings to light its potential value: a useful metaphor for that which we non-farmers might first perceive as something "bad" and something to be avoided. After we get past the initial discomfort, we can often experience its value. Don't you think? ====JACK: What a great example! "Milorganite" is the result of the City of Milwaukee turning a waste product into a money-maker.

FROM TARMART REV: When I experience "the bad" earlier on w/o much embarrassment and consequence . . . it becomes a "good thing" later when tempted to do it all over again . . . I just smile within and think to myself . . . "been there, done that and not falling again for it!!" I'm not going to tell you what they were, Jack . . . I'll keep you guessing!! ====JACK: You prove the truth of the quote..."Every saint has a past, and every sinner has a future."

FROM SHARIN' SHARON: Worry is my something bad. I know Jesus says not to worry that God gives us everything we need and people constantly advise me not to worry and to have faith and that makes me worry about my worrying and lacking faith. The worry doesn't seem to become good but the fact that it drives me to seek God, over and over and over again, and low-and-behold God always seems to come-by-here and provide for me and others so actually experiencing that so consistently--what an awesome God we have!!!!!!!!even worry becomes more and more like a little puppy nipping at my heels. I keep getting stronger and stronger and I think actually being able to "reframe" difficulties so pretty much all the time the bad morphs into good seemingly inevitably--the arc bends towards justice in the world--God's Kingdom.====JACK: Keep on paying attention to Jesus.

FROM GOOD DEBT JON: I believe my 2006 heart attack, or myocardial infarction if you prefer, set me on a path to eventually lose 60 pounds and seek healthy eating habits. Though I waited about five years to get serious about it. The event caused a bit of hopelessness, apathy, procrastination, and then eventually the correct response. I am as Winston Churchill once said of Americans, "After exhausting every other possibility, they eventually do the right thing."====JACK: If some had said to you, "Do you want to have a heart attack?" you probably would have emphatically responded, "NO!" Sometimes the good is wrapped up in the bad.

FROM BLAZING OAKS: As John Steinbeck wrote, "What good is the warmth of summer, without the cold of winter to give it sweetness?" The good is twice as appreciated after something bad has happened. I've read many, many stories which pointed out how something "bad" turned out to be a blessing, and have experienced this myself, as when I was "let go" from difficult middle school teaching position in a downsize, when I didn't yet have tenure, only to be hired to teach in a great school system, where I was much happier, and stayed over 20 years! What seemed a catastrophe, became a real blessing! And I met my BFF at that school..====JACK: The movie, "It's A Wonderful Life," is another example..

FROM OUTHOUSE JUDY: Most of my bads have been turned into blessings. In fact, I can't really name one that hasn't.====JACK: You and St. Paul seem to be in the same boat.

FROM HS IN ILLINOIS: Jack, on this subject, Romans 8:28 is a good word.====JACK:: Romans 8:28....'And we know that in all things God works for the good of those who love him ." Ahh, One of my favorites!

Jack's Winning Words 12/27/13

"When there's snow on the ground I like to pretend that I'm walking on clouds." (Ikkaku, Hosaka & Kawabata) Pretending is lots of fun. Sometimes it's a child's game. At other times it can make the adult world tolerable. One of the favorite Beatles' songs is, "Imagine." What are some of your imaginations? The Fiddler sang, "If I were a rich man..." Pretend that you'd won the lottery. How would that affect you?   ;-) Jack

FROM HAPPY TRAILS IN NOVA SCOTIA: I did win the lottery, in 1966—I went to church and found Hannelore====JACK: I agree! What were the odds of finding someone like her?====HT: one in several billion, providing only one can meet all of them====JACK: Once you find the "pearl of great price," you stop digging.

FROM MICHIZONA RAY: The good thing about having what one needs, is that one might take advantage of the opportunity to cease from seeking more. Once one has everything, (s)he has the opportunity to understand its vanity first-hand. If one already has one winter coat, would winning two more make that person any warmer? Those of us who have been blessed with much, can do much through that with which we have been blessed. We have already won the lottery of sorts, and now we get to share the blessings in a variety of ways! By the way, I don't look to our government for charity by legislation; nor for its involvement that corrupts what it touches. I think it better to "look to the hills" for the Spirit of Charity and the guidance of its fruitful direction. But, that's just my opinion. ====JACK: When "common" charity does not reach the needy, the government (all of us) steps in to help...Social Security, Medicare, FEMA, food stamps, etc. Most of us give to charity, but few give "until it hurts." There was a Japanese Christian, Kagawa, who was known for never having a shirt on his back. Whenever he was given a shirt for himself, he'd give it away to someone who was needier than he was. Even if I won the lottery, I doubt that I would use it in the way that Kagawa would.====RAY: As much as it was originally intended, the government is not "us" by any stretch of a wish that it were. If the government has to "step in" to provide what has not otherwise been provided, it is because of a lack of Charity; it is in no way an extension of it. It is by the cunning of deceit that the charitable people rely on the government for what has been conveyed to be charity. Just like the Pharisees, whose works were corrupted by their own spirit that served its own purpose, so does our government parallel the same. I suppose if I were to believe that Justice comes from the Law or the Courts, I might also believe that charity comes from the government. I don't think it is even close to being possible; but that's just my opinion.====JACK: Like it, or not...perfect, or imperfect...the government is us. That's what democracy is all about. The Representatives are called representatives, because they represent us. As an aside, do you think elected officials should vote "their knowledge of an issue," or should they vote according to the polling of their constituency?====RAY: They haven't represented me for many years, I have written many times about how I preferred to be represented by them, and without exception, their responses have been with regard to what they think. I have clearly been in the minority. Nonetheless, I have never been able to understand how so many are so easily and repeatedly led astray by these who deceive for their election to office and for their sense of power. We are a democratic republic, and as such, the imperfections of the system might be held at bay a little longer than a simple democracy. But in time, and without correction, the damage takes hold. I only wish my "representatives" did indeed represent me. They don't. Frankly, they cannot whilst they believe that God can be separated from them, us, and me. To the issue of today's WW though: Charity is the work of the Church, by its members, who are members of the Body of Christ. We are His "representatives"; and to my mind, expecting "someone else" (like a government) to be and do charitable service is an abomination to what Charity truly is. Caesar confiscates the first fruits of our work through our taxed wages. Can you imagine if the religious organizations did the same with what is otherwise our tithe? Would either "contribution" be considered "free-will" offerings? I would say not. Charity cannot be forced upon us; nor can it be deferred to a government. I will not stand before God when He asks what I have done with my talents and claim governmental programs as my service. If so, I expect I will be cast away just like the servant who buried his talent in the same way. ====JACK: The voters elect their representative. That's how democracy works. Each representative has a designated constituency. It is impossible to think that the one elected can vote, pleasing everyone who has voted...and not voted..

 FROM BLAZING OAKS: I JUST READ YOUR MENTION OF KAGAWA IN TODAY'S WW, AND REMEMBER WHEN HE WAS A LEADER AT THE AB NATIONAL CONVENTION. SUCH A HUMBLE MAN. I REMEMBER HIS SAYING, "IT SAYS IN THE BIBLE THAT "JESUS WENT ABOUT DOING GOOD. I AM

HUMBLED THAT I AM SO EASILY CONTENT TO JUST GO ABOUT...." HE PUT US ALL TO SHAME!!====JACK: ....and he had to show his Christian love, often in an hostile environment.

FROM TARMART REV: "I can only imagine!!"====JACK: Do you mean that you've never bought a lottery ticket?====REV: True story . . . Stopped for gas on a Sunday afternoon here in Willmar several years ago now . . . after I filled up, the cashier gave me a lottery ticket as they were giving one per fill-up or over so many gallons of gas . . . I asked him if he would explain how it works . . . he scratched it of for me and it said I got a free one . . . he thus gave me another, scratched it off again for me and behold I won $50.00 . . . I was so greedy I forgot to give him a tip . . . so officially I'm way ahead of the game . . . to the best of knowledge, I did buy one in West Bloomfield, thinking maybe God had given me the numbers in my sleep, finding out later it was the winning numbers from the time before. That's it. I heard a message on it one day explaining one could only win at the loss of countless others. I believe he called it coveting?!?! I'm now waiting for the next dream!!

FROM TRIHARDER: Actually, it was John Lennon without the Beatles.====JACK: Picky, picky! But, I guess that goes with being a lawyer.
FROM PASTY PAT: I'd have to be really careful to save a little for my travel fund because otherwise I'd give it all away.====JACK: Would you splurge and travel first-class?

FROM MOLINER JT: Interesting thought. I don't believe anyone "knows" how they would be affected by a big winning. It wouldn't affect me at all, because I don't play any lotteries. However, it's fun to dream. ====JACK: You never win, if you never play. Of course, you never lose, either. The odds of winning the recent mega-lottery were about 1 in 259 million.

FROM CALUMET BOB: Keweenaw County reports 141 inches have fallen thus far. The clouds are thick up here.====JACK: With that much snow, you're walking in the clouds.

FROM RI IN BOSTON: Little children are so easily satisfied...the simplest sort of "let's pretend" becomes exciting for them. They get a lot of enjoyment from being "frightened" when they know the so-called monster scaring them is granddad. To comment on winning the lottery, that good luck becomes double jeopardy...after you have the money, to find a safe way to hold on to it, or if you're giving it away, to distribute it prudently to some really deserving recipients. In my situation now I'm satisfied with the status quo.====JACK: Before a building can be designed, it has to be imagined. Even God has to be imagined. Winning the lottery is wishful thinking. Actually winning it can turn out to be a nightmare.

Thursday, December 26, 2013

Jack's Winning Words 12/26/13

"Peace is the first thing the angels sang." (John Keble) What do you think the angels were singing about when they used the words, "Peace on earth, good will to all?" What does peace mean to you? No war? No fighting? Stillness? Harmony? Contentment? Reconciliation? Calm? No arguing? No bullying? Or is it a peace that passes all understanding?

Think about that as you sing, "Hark! The herald angels..."   ;-) Jack

FROM TARMART REV: "Peace" in the midst of war, fighting, stillness, harmony, contentment, reconciliation, calm, argument and bullying...a certain peace that passeth all understanding! Oh! to be gifted with a greater amount this coming year would be my New Year resolution.====JACK: "Let there be be peace on earth, and let it begin with me," is a good resolution.

FROM HONEST JOHN: "wholeness"====JACK: Would you explain what you mean by, wholeness? My holiday brain is a bit slow today.====JOHN: No longer half a person because of the alienation from God====JACK: I like the song, *We are one in the Spirit, We are one in the Lord*"....which makes us whole.====JOHN: The wholeness with God promotes whole ness with All.====JACK: Does it help that I buy some groceries at Whole Foods occasionally?

FROM SHARIN' SHARON: Knowing that I belong to God. I always did want to belong somewhere and have grown into understanding that I belong to God and He accepts me as I am.====JACK: Everyone belongs to the Creator, but not everyone knows where they come from. Peace can bring closure...Now, I know! In Sunday School we used to sing a song that had this chorus..."Now I belong to Jesus, Jesus belongs to me, Not for the years of time alone, But for eternity."

FROM MICHIZONA RAY: It seems to me that Jesus' commandment to love one another as we are loved by Him, sets a standard for what Love truly is - rather than what I might otherwise believe it to be. Within this state of love, which is by its nature absent a focus of oneself, a peace within (in an experiential way) accompanies the love that is provided for another. For when the concern for oneself becomes absent in the love for another, how could there be any experience of oneself? ====JACK: So...if there's love for one another, there will peace?====RAY: I think this would be so. For does it not also follow that where there is no Love, there can be also no Peace? And, further, the world knows of turmoil, anxieties, lust for power, the desirable avoidance of Freedom, the idolatry of things, etc., all of which bring an absence of Peace. This we, as mankind, can claim as something we have experienced first-hand. So, if we know the fruit of the aforementioned brings no peace, would it not then be a wiser venture to pursue peace through its polarity, Love? In the biblical sense, Jesus brings Light to the darkness, and the same Light dwells within those who believe in Him and who follow Him, which is the Light, the Way, and the Life. When the Light (Love) comes to the world otherwise blinded in darkness, the angels sing a song of Peace on earth.====JACK: It's sorta like in The Blues Brothers movie, when Jake shouts, "YES! YES! JESUS... I HAVE SEEN THE LIGHT!"

FROM MKH IN MICHIGAN: True Peace...must mean all of those things... A peace that surpasses all understanding!====JACK: True peace is like trying to explain true love. Words don't do it justice.

Tuesday, December 24, 2013

Jack's Winning Words 12/24/13

"I will honor Christmas in my heart and try to keep it all year."
(Charles Dickens) What does it mean, to keep Christmas? Dickens', A
Christmas Carol, seems to indicate that "Christmas" is having sympathy
for the poor. Early critics saw the story as an indictment of the rich
taking advantage of the poor. Perhaps the way to honor Christmas is by
being an advocate for the poor. Pope Francis appears to like the idea.
;-) Jack

 FROM MICHIZONA RAY: For myself, Christmas is the Light that has been
brought to the darkness. For me, the Light in this sense applies to all who
are poor-in-spirit. Whether they are rich or poor in the world is a
different matter -- a fruit of Grace not of spirit. For one can be poor in
the world but not poor in one's spirit; just as one can be rich in the world
and still poor-in-spirit (as we note in Scrooge). Scrooge's redemption was
first in his spirit, the fruit of which brought generosity. We need to feed
with food for the body and even more by the spirit....This is what the
reminder of Christmas brings to the mind of my soul. ====JACK: Thanks
for the reminder that even the rich can be poor. The word poverty has
more than one application.

 FROM RI IN BOSTON: The year-end holidays are always a time when
charities inflict our mailbox with overload. Some are genuinely hard-
working organizations, with programs devoted to giving food and shelter
to the poor, the down-and-out, the destitute, so I support several of
them throughout the year. The Christmas season seems to provide more
exposure than usual to the plight of so many indigent people, and during

the holidays when I'm sharing so much cheer, I'm unable to hold back giving more, hoping to lift the spirit of those in need, even a little bit. There's an aphorism that comes to mind: "There but for the grace of God go I." A "hearty" Christmas to you Pastor Freed, and to all who share your WW.====JACK: The mail requests to "help the needy" are many at this time of the year, but the plight of the poor continues throughout the year.

FRO TARMART REV: "Blessed are the poor in spirit: for theirs is the kingdom of heaven." . . . Always bringing out "the preacher" in me, Jack!====JACK: You're the second one to remind me that there is a "poorness" beyond the economic kind.

FROM HONEST JOHN: I love A Christmas Carol. My sister Jean read it ti me when I was a little boy. Still watch it almost every year. God bless us everyone.====JACK: We can appreciate the fact that there were stories about Christmas before "Rudolph" and "The Grinch."

FROM SHARIN' SHARON: For me, more and more, Christmas is a time for empathy for everyone experiencing changes in their families. Talked to my mother-in-law yesterday in assisted living in another state and she seemed a bit down--other residents have their families right there and can go out somewhere. Talked to a friend here whose son divorced his wife this year and she was trying to arrange a happy Christmas celebration time together with the grandson. Guess these are the poor-in-spirit. My prayers are for those in our society who have never had money for Christmas as well as those who have had joy in Christmases past and now, due to job loss, etc. are also coping with a no-money Christmas but the wonderful thing, in spite of the problems, is that all of these people know deep down that Christmas is somehow a different kind of day, I believe that many of them know that Christmas holds our sorrow, as well as our joy, our sorrow that the world does not yet know Christmas and that we live in the midst of all that and can only turn to God who I think and believe is coming into each of our lives every day with some little miracle of His Love and Encouragement, some little Birth of New Faith in the Baby Jesus, that is my hope anyway.====JACK: We sing in one of our carols..."The hopes and fears of all the years are met in Thee...." That is THE hope!

 FROM FACEBOOK LIZ: I am asking Santa for a good economy & jobs galore for everyone..... ====JACK: I think that Santa's in the toy business. But, who knows? Maybe he's branched out.

Monday, December 23, 2013

Jack's Winning Words 12/23/13
"Another belief of mine is that everyone else my age is an adult, whereas I am merely in disguise." (Margaret Atwood) A young mom, who enjoys playing with her children, wrote, "I keep trying to fit in with the grown-up crowd." Do you fit in with the crowd that's your age? When I was younger and being silly, I was told, "Act your age!" Is it silly to want to hop and skip and to stand in line to talk with Santa?   ;-)

Jack

 FROM HONEST JOHN: Be yourself.   Do, within reason, what you like. Don't pretend you are young just to impress others.====JACK: You were (are) a good children's story teller, because you know when and how to be a child.

 FROM TARMART REV: I played Santa while there in West Bloomfield and working with Parks & Rec . . . Enjoyed bringing a smile to those elderly ladies' faces (they could no longer "hop and skip", but they were eager to sit on Santa's lap!!====JACK: I wonder what would happen if you sat in your usual place at Target and Walmart wearing a Santa suit?

 ====REV: I could most likely get away with, but if a former Lutheran pastor sat on my lap...we'd both make the front page of the paper.====JACK: I'm staying in Michigan.

 FROM PEPPERMINT MARY: i like to sit at the kids table.====JACK: I do, too. But, I've never thought to ask for their permission. Or, can they see through my disguise and see me as one of them? ====MARY: i don't ask permission either. maybe they do know where we belong. it's nice to think so!

 FROM MICHIZONA RAY: I suppose "acting" one's age is just an act anyway; so it seems best to be your "developed" age, or honest, or just as you are. If one "acts" like someone long enough, (s)he might start to believe (s)he is who (s)he pretends to be. What a tragedy! It seems that as we "act our age" we lose that something in ourselves that is willing to run through the sprinkler with or without clothes on. I think I like the "kids table" too. They are more likely to be honest and just themselves.====JACK: I remember once when we were at a church member's house. Our kids were playing with their kids. Our son (about 10) took a bread stick pretzel and pretended that he was Groucho Marx. The other father reprimanded him for playing with his food. I thought that what David did was pretty funny. We still laugh at the event of kids being kids.

 FROM WATERFORD JAN: Sometimes it is amusing to see someone "act" like a kid to entertain others, or even make a serious point in a memorable way. To watch an adult try to "be" younger than their age is sometimes uncomfortable. I'm wonder if our Winning Words author is asking for our permission for him to "hop and skip and to stand in line to talk with Santa?" I think that would be a charming sight to see! ====JACK: One of my favorite comedians was Jonathan Winters. He always seemed to have fun doing silly stuff. BTW, have you ever seen the Monty Python skit about the Silly Walk? It's on Youtube.

 FROM SBP IN FLORIDA: For me, today's WW tags into Eric Berne's theory that the facets of personalities are basically Parent, Adult, Child...PAC..and our responses to life's situations reflect one or the other or a combination of these facets. (An over-simplification, of course.) And..Yes! My "child" is reflected in "silly" situations or pranks or self-indulgence wistful memories....I think that it is good to allow my "child" to pop up every once in a while. It makes me smile at me.====JACK:

Winning Words allows me to reveal several facets...friend, pastor, philosopher and nostalgiaist.

FROM KF IN MICHIGAN: "It takes a long time to grow young" (Picasso) ====JACK: Now...that one, I like. Some of P's paintings seem almost child-like.

Friday, December 20, 2013

Jack's Winning Words 12/20/13

"It's better to walk alone than with a crowd going the wrong direction." (Diane Grant) Raising a child is risky business. So many "what if-s..." Dr. Spock, well known for his advice to parents, said, "You know more than you think you do." Think back to when you were the age of your child. You remember "the red flags." Among the reddest was hanging out with the wrong crowd. Even as adults, choose friends wisely.   ;-) Jack

FROM PH IN MINNESOTA: i also like this one: stand for something or you will fall for anything.. ====JACK: Some think that in the Lutheran liturgy people stand and sit and stand and sit in order to keep from falling asleep.====PH: he reminds me of Gene Robinson in the Presbyterian (?) tradition. by the way, have you seen the video The Bible Tells Me So. it is quite good. i think you can even view it online. Daniel Karslake is the producer/director. it won a bunch of awards when it first came out in 2007. its all about the gay/lesbian debate.====JACK: The Church seems to be a debating society as each generation comes of age. From the very beginning...life is a matter of choices, and those choices, so often, depend on how God's "Word" is interpreted in a changing society.====PH you are so right. look at the following issues over which the church ended up doing an about-face. the Salem Witch trials, Spanish Inquisition, human slavery in the UK and the USA, segregation in the south, inter-racial marriage, women being ordained, divorced clergy serving again in the pulpit, Galileo and Copernicus, limbo, mandatory celibacy, purgatory, suicide, etc. the church has often changed its mind radically over these and many other issues.

 FROM LP IN PLYMOUTH: Hm... I like your point. Somehow I needed that :)====JACK: "Birds of a feather flock together." There are many saying like that. Teaching children how to choose wisely is a very important responsibility.====LP Actually needed reminding for myself. I keep trying to 'fit in' with the grown-up 'in' crowd and just don't. Maybe it's time to let that be OK.====JACK: One of my favorite poems is by Douglas Malloch. I especially like the last line.
 If you can't be a pine on the top of the hill
Be a scrub in the valley--but be
The best little scrub by the side of the rill;
Be a bush if you can't be a tree.
If you can't be a bush be a bit of the grass,
And some highway some happier make;
If you can't be a muskie then just be a bass--
But the liveliest bass in the lake!
We can't all be captains, we've got to be crew,
There's something for all of us here.

There's big work to do and there's lesser to do,

And the task we must do is the near.

If you can't be a highway then just be a trail,

If you can't be the sun be a star;

It isn't by size that you win or you fail--

Be the best of whatever you are!

FROM HONEST JOHN: A lot of people are choosing not to hang out with the ELCA right now.   Are we the "wrong crowd?"====JACK: We are choosing every day. That's why G-d created us to have free-will. ====JOHN: Some of us consistently choose to avoid the issue.....I did ask a question.   Do you have a response?====JACK: I happen to think that I'm going in the right direction with the right crowd. As with all choices, I could be right and I could be wrong, but the choice is mine to make, and I've made it.

FROM SHARIN' SHARON: this is so true. Among adults I know who have gotten into trouble and then gone to prison, it seems like the hardest thing for them to do is to learn not to go back to their habitual ways of making friends, i.e., stay away from the bars and so forth. I know Jesus always hung out in such places but we vulnerable people probably need most of all to hang out with people who go to church. Probably too simplistic, but I've known a few people who've gotten into trouble with the law and shed a few tears over it, worrying about how to be of help to them.====JACK: One of my first Winning Words was this one. "Virtue is learned at mother's knee. Vice is learned at other joints." That's simplistic, too, but the truth is that good and bad friends are everywhere. Discernment is the key.

 FROM TARMART REV: Interesting thought . . . fully agree . . . however, it was our Savior who felt it not necessary to remain equal with God, but gave up His privilege and came to earth to walk along side us who walking the wrong direction (Phil 2:5-7) . . . I'm sure you have joined Him and myself as well in walking along side some of these traveling the wrong direction during your lifetime, for a distance anyway? 0;-) ====JACK: Life is such that we walk among all kinds of people. I remember my children saying to me, when they were in high school..."We know who the druggies are." Life is the choices we make.

 FROM MICHIZONA RAY: I have been reading Habakkuk, and his reference to the twisted stick seems to apply here. A twisted stick can be twisted in many various directions; but a straight stick is straight in only one way. Just as today, there are many ways to be misled, and many who will mislead. I think it is Faith in its fullest sense to which Habakkuk refers. And, we can't be the "best" parents, we only need to be "good enough" parents. ====JACK: I think that most of us are twisted sticks. Eventually, by the grace of God, we can "straighten out."   BTW, that's a good Habakkuk reference.

 FROM FACEBOOK LIZ: there is usually someone else to walk with you...====JACK: I went back to examine the lyrics to "You'll never walk alone." I thought to ask the question..."Who will you walk with?"

 FROM HR IN MICHIGAN: It's tough to walk alone. There needs to be a sense of real confidence in the direction to head for someone to not go with the crowd. The level of self doubt is always amplified when you consider going it alone especially against conventional wisdom. Your thinking is considered suspect, your actions mocked or dismissed out of hand. Your called names or worse. It ain't easy, that's why most people take the easy road.====JACK: I think that Robert Frost understood that point when he wrote, "The Road Not Taken."

TWO roads diverged in a yellow wood,

And sorry I could not travel both

And be one traveler, long I stood

And looked down one as far as I could

To where it bent in the undergrowth;

Then took the other, as just as fair,

And having perhaps the better claim,

Because it was grassy and wanted wear;

Though as for that the passing there

Had worn them really about the same,

And both that morning equally lay

In leaves no step had trodden black.

Oh, I kept the first for another day!

Yet knowing how way leads on to way,

I doubted if I should ever come back.

I shall be telling this with a sigh

Somewhere ages and ages hence:

Two roads diverged in a wood, and I—

I took the one less traveled by,

And that has made all the difference.

FROM HCC CHUCK: AMEN to that. we inherited from Lois parents a stone carving (very heavy) carved by Lois's father's uncle who lived in the coal mining area of central Penna on it is engraved "WATCH YOUR FRIENDS" I wish I knew the story behind the message.====JACK: Some messages are left for us to interpret...just like with the Scriptures. By responding to today's Winning Words you've given your own interpretation...and it seems to fit..

Thursday, December 19, 2013

Jack's Winning Words 12/19/13

"To me, life is about helping people." (Ernie Banks) Do you have an all-time baseball hero? Mine is Mr. Sunshine, called that because of his upbeat disposition. Today's quote came as he received the Presidential Medal of Freedom. At this time of the year much emphasis is placed on helping people. For Ernie, it was a year-round passion. The Bible says that the "needy" are always around us. Look for opportunities to help. ;-) Jack

FROM HONEST JOHN: We share Ernie as our baseball hero.   I still have a plastic statue of him that I got at Wrigley as a kid.   Met Gene Baker at an EM ball game that he was scouting.====JACK: Thinking back to the time when I was growing up with the Cubs....It didn't seem like there was so much emphasis on winning as there is today. We still wanted our team to win, but the "intensity" seemed less. I wonder if had something to do with the fact that players stayed with the club for longer periods of time (no free agency). It was baseball, not money-ball. "Our" generation can relate to the *Field of Dreams*.

FROM GOOD DEBT JON: Amen.====JACK: Your Amen must relate to "helping the needy," since someone from Ohio might not be familiar with a Chicago Cubs' player.====JON: You are correct. I agree heartily with Ernie's sentiment.====JACK::Some ballplayers are more than ballplayers.

 FROM TARMART REV: Will do, Jack . . . maybe I can share a bag of popcorn with an unexpected recipient this afternoon . . . I'll tell them my friend, Jack, suggested I do so!!   I do have, as last year, $1000.00 donated by three of us to pass out to un-expecting folk to brighten their Christmas spirit. So far, we've blessed three or four single mothers with temporary housing, car repair and Christmas money to purchase gifts for them and their children. Our church has a yearly anonymous donor (known only to the staff) who has given $10,000 the past several Christmases . . .the church matches that as well . . . and we choose deserving individuals and families to bless this Christmas season. It is very enjoyable to be part of such a giving church in this manner.====JACK: From a bag of popcorn to $10,000...every little bit helps. There is so much need. Every little bit helps. In Sunday School we used to sing: "Jesus bids us shine with a clear pure light, like a little candle burning in the night. In this world of darkness, we must shine. You, in your small corner, and I in mine." Your candle is shining at Target and Walmart.

 FROM CK IN MICHIGAN: I grew up with the Cubs of old! Earnie Banks, Glen Beckert, Don Kessinger and Ron Santo! Around the horn for the Cubs infield ! I am still a Cubby fan to this day! Thanks for the memory you gave me today of a simpler time and and a great message for every day! Enjoy Jack! ;-) ====JACK: I've been a Tigers fan for longer than I was a Cubs fan, but you never seem to forget the team you cheered for when you were a kid. I used to cut the pictures of the Cubs' players out of the newspaper and put them in a scrapbook. Whatever happened to that scrapbook with pictures of Ernie and the rest? We once stayed in a condo in Florida that belonged to Don Kessinger.

 FROM RI IN BOSTON: If all mankind would commit to those simple WW we probably wouldn't have those "needy" people anymore.====jJACK
If!!!!! I'm reminded of the Kipling poem, IF.
If you can keep your head when all about you
Are losing theirs and blaming it on you;
If you can trust yourself when all men doubt you,
But make allowance for their doubting too:
If you can wait and not be tired by waiting,
Or, being lied about, don't deal in lies,
Or being hated don't give way to hating,
And yet don't look too good, nor talk too wise;

If you can dream---and not make dreams your master;
If you can think---and not make thoughts your aim,
If you can meet with Triumph and Disaster
And treat those two impostors just the same:.
If you can bear to hear the truth you've spoken
Twisted by knaves to make a trap for fools,

Or watch the things you gave your life to, broken,

And stoop and build'em up with worn-out tools;

If you can make one heap of all your winnings

And risk it on one turn of pitch-and-toss,

And lose, and start again at your beginnings,

And never breathe a word about your loss:

If you can force your heart and nerve and sinew

To serve your turn long after they are gone,

And so hold on when there is nothing in you

Except the Will which says to them: "Hold on!"

 ====RI Kipling's poem calls out so many of the hardships or injustices with which we are confronted in life. It challenges the dignity that is often dormant within us.====JACK: Kipling saw the "need" through his eyes. You see it through yours, and I see it through mine. The question is....What do we do about it?

 FROM SHARIN' SHARON: Enjoyed the WW and the poem IF. Our prayer group was praying up at the church on Wednesday morning and especially praying for the concerns of the people who use our food pantry. They write them on little pieces of paper. Was praying for each of them to receive blessings of health, peace and prosperity and it came to mind that, even though it seems daunting to believe that people at the margins financially can feel prosperous yet nevertheless being blessed by God is in the eyes of the beholder and praying for each person to have that window opened where a blessing is poured on them of some sort of wealth that is "exactly what they want and feel they need at THAT TIME" so that they can go on, like in the poem IF. I appreciate your blogging the poem. Thanks and God bless you.====JACK: Sometimes, just mentioned the name of someone in need is enough of a prayer. God knows and understands. ====SHARON: I appreciated your comment to my comment. Sometimes, when I'm praying through the little pieces of paper, I get discouraged because they are all people who I never meet and actually relate conversationally with, but I still doggedly insist to myself that-- even though there is only a little piece of paper between us--they must never remain anonymous people and have names--your comment was so comforting. At Emmanuel, we care in a personal way for the people who use our pantry. ====JACK: The hymn, There's A Wideness in God's Mercy, has this verse...

If our love were but more simple,

We should take Him at His word;

And our lives would be all sunshine

In the sweetness of our Lord.

Sometimes we make our prayers more complex than they need to be.

 FROM TRIHARDER: Never won a world series. He might have been perceived to be a "much greater" player had he played on either coast and received the coverage of a Willie Mays. A shortstop with 500+ home runs!====JACK: Maybe his greatest days were when he played for the Kansas City Monarchs. ====TH: In terms of records, there should be two eras for baseball (and other sports, but particularly baseball because it is so record oriented). To have excluded an entire class of people from a sport and to include records that were set without participation of those people is basically using records from an inferior league.====JACK:

During the "Before Jackie Robinson Era," I wonder which league was the "major" league?====TH: Great question. It's too bad that no real records were kept. I do love the legends. Cool Papa Bell was so fast he once hit a line drive through the pitcher's legs and it hit him in the ass as he was sliding into second base.====Now, that's fast. Satchel Paige, in the major leagues, was an anachronism. His "prime" was before he sat in the bullpen in a rocking chair.====TH I wanted to write a book about the Negro Leagues. I started to do research. A very paltry library; very few references.====JACK: Everybody knows of Jackie Robinson, but have you heard of Lou Carinio and Lon Cherban?

FROM BBC IN ILLINOIS: Met him with my son a year ago in a skybox; Ernie's still a gracious gentleman. Thanks for sharing his quote.====JACK: I've only had the chance to admire him from a far, not from a skybox .

FROM OUTHOUSE JUDY: It's easy to find someone to help lately.====JACK: It's surprising how, so many in need will help one another. That's a major untold story.

FROM SB IN MICHIGAN: Thank you for helping people daily with your "Winning Words."====JACK: We each do our thing. God has a way of making your thing and mine work out.

FROM AW IN ILLINOIS: He is one of my favorites.   Good quote. Thanks.====JACK: When he's introduced, the announcer will often say, "Here he is, everybody's favorite, Mr. Cub." He's truly someone who needs no more introduction than that====AW: .Seems the coach came to Ron and Said...Pack up, we are going to play an exhibition game in Virgina. Santo said: No Way. I don't have to go and I won't. Coach said ..yes you will. It is in your contract. Santo said, we shall see, and he refered to his attorney. After a day, the Attourney called and said: "Yes, Santo, there is a Virginia clause!". (get the pun?)

FROM FM IN WISCONSIN: Thanks for the word today – I too always liked Ernie, and will attempt to heed your thoughts about looking for opportunities to help, not only in the approaching season of Christmas, but year around.====JACK: Jesus, indeed, is new every day, so, in truth, every day is Christmas.

FROM ME IN NEWPORT BEACH: I agree. He and Cal Ripken rank up there in my book. I was at the game when Cal R broke Lou Gehrig's iron man record and later met him serendipitously in a hotel in Seattle where he was preparing to do a night ball game. From my perspective, a very humble man, as, it appears is Ernie Banks.====JACK: Sparky Anderson, when he was manger of the Detroit Tigers, used to attend a Catholic Church where the priest was a friend of mine. He encouraged worshippers to let Sparky worship as an ordinary person. He was truly a humble person and a regular church attender.

FROM JE IN MICHIGAN: This is so absolutely perfect for today. Today, a group of colleagues and I gave wrapped gifts and gift cards to a family with five children. Husband lost his job; they are now paying insurance for family of seven, plus house payment, gas, etc... She called me in desperation two weeks ago. I did our usual checks and balances and then called her back to ask her to send us the kids' "wish" lists. We got everything. She was completely overwhelmed. I had Christmas ahead of time today as the mother came to pick up gifts and hugged each of us.====JACK: One of the Christmas carols goes...."Love came down at Christmas." You and your friends made that song come true for a family.

FROM ML IN MICHIGAN: My husband said you probably know the Ernie banks famous quote, "Let's play two!"====JACK: Anybody who knows Ernie knows that quote. He loved baseball so much that he didn't mind playing doubleheaders. When you love your work, it's not work.

FROM BLAZING OAKS: Ah, memories! My mother's all time favorite player, and she was a die-hard Cub fan! Christmas is certainly the time we help people. My Angel tree person was a 3 yr. old. just delivered clothes and toys on her list today, including "Princess Shoes"...:-) And our Neighborhood House, and the school across from our church (a mitten, scarf and hat tree in the Narthex) etcl. etc. Ernie is so right. "In the air there's a feeling of Christmas"!====JACK: Some people keep their good habits for a lifetime. I wonder who it was that set the example for Ernie?

FROM SBP IN FLORIDA: Life IS about helping people! It requires taking care of yourself so that you can continue to be of help ....in many ways to others. Baseball! My Dad and I used to go to "night" games at Browning Field...local teams. And we'd listen to the games on the radio....better than TV. Just a couple names come up at this point and I,m not certain...White Sox or Cubs....Gabby Hartnett, Bob Feller, Enos Slaughter??? I like "If"....hadn't thought about it for a long time. I'm wondering why I could find only one reference to Kipling,s "If" in Bartlett,s....and it was negative! ====JACK: I posted "If" on the blog, so you don't have to rely on Bartlett for a judgment. And, then...you have to know something about the context of the poem and why it was written. Theb same goes for passages from the Bible. BTW, "Gabby" was a nickname, because he talked so much. Feller was called, Rapid Robert, because of his fastball. Slaughter had the nickname of "Country" for a somewhat obvious reason. Did you have a nickname?

Wednesday, December 18, 2013

Jack's Winning Words 12/18/13

"You've got to be a thermostat rather than a thermometer." (Cornel West) I don't know about your house, but at ours the thermostat gets quite a workout...up and down. That gadget is used to make the house comfortable. Cornel's words say that we can be a kind of thermostat in the world around us, cooling down situations, or adding warmth when there's a chilliness among people. A smile and kind words might do it. ;-) Jack

FROM MK IN MICHIGAN: Thank you for touching my life every morning with your winning words. ====JACK: Your response is a good day-starter.

FROM LS IN MICHIGAN: Right on - I was just talking about this subject ! Sweet your quote was right on And I practice this ====JACK: There's a button on the thermostat marked, HOLD. Hold that smile and those kind words.

FROM RI IN BOSTON: At our house we are a thermocouple...two dissimilar components that are joined together for sensing heat between them.====JACK" The first time I heard about a thermocouple was when our furnace had a problem. The repairman explained it to me, and it made sense. Some "explanations" could help with family problems, too.

AFROM PEPPERMINT MARY: a day in a life...====JACK: A life is made up of single days. It's usually the people who appear in those days that make them significant.

FROM TARMART REV: You've got my vote and attention, Jack . . . ready for a lunch at Wal-Mart and popcorn later in the afternoon at Target thermosetting!====JACK: Fresh popcorn is a great snack, but it's even better when shared with someone else.

FROM BBC IN ILLINOIS: Love Dr. West. Used to listen to him often on the Tavis Smiley show in the afternoon on the radio; now they've gone on television I think so I miss the provocative conversations. ====JACK: Provocative conversation doesn't seem to sell products, so we're left with Honey Boo Boo.

FROM INDY GENIE: Wow...good one. (My home thermostat gets a work out too:)====JACK: Before thermostats, my parents would say to me, "Go down and put some more coal in the furnace, it feels cold in here."

FROM BLAZING OAKS: As Geo. Sanders expressed at his Syracuse U. Commencement Address :"What I regret most in my life are failures of kindness." In a Spouse, Friend, profession associate, etc. kindness is such an asset!! Or as Bennet Cerf once opined: "A pat on the back, though only a few vertebrae removed from a kick in the pants, is miles ahead in its results". Enuff said! :-)====JACK: A pat on the back side these days can sometimes get you into a lot of trouble.

FROM OUTHOUSE JUDY: We have to be like a Michigander...our weather flexs up and down...from warm to cold to cool to heat. If we could adjust our weather would our thermostat be at 70, 80 perhaps 65? A thermometer does come in handy for making sure our temperature doesn't get too high.====JACK: Goldilocks had the right idea. She found the porridge that was just right.

FROM DMF IN MINNESOTA: I like this one.====JACK: Ahhhhh! Just right!

Tuesday, December 17, 2013

Jack's Winning Words 12/17/13

"Oh, that I had wings like a dove, for then I would fly away and be at rest." (Psalm 55:6) The dove is one of 34 different birds mentioned in the Bible. The Lord's care for creation is illustrated in the passage..."not even a sparrow falls to the ground, but that God is aware and cares." He's aware of your situation, too, and cares. 110 years ago, today, Orville Wright emulated the birds by "flying" 120 feet for 12 seconds. ;-) Jack

FROM HONEST JOHN: We're going out to the Wright's shop on Friday evening...Greenfield Village Christmas Walk.====JACK: The life of Henry Ford has received mixed reviews. In that respect, he's like many of us. One of the good things that Ford did was to make sure that some of important Americana was preserved at Greenfield Village. Preserving the actual Wright Brother's bike shop is just one example. Thanks Henry!

FROM RI IN BOSTON: Birds on the wing are such a spectacle. This morning at the breakfast table, out the window we saw a flock of geese in V-formation heading south. They were elegant and precisely spaced. It must have been the sudden change to bitter weather here that nudged them to finally get moving southward. The Wright brothers headed south too, determined to give themselves wings. They put in all the work to make it into the air and stay there, while today we essentially take these huge airliners for granted. Regarding that historic first flight in 1903, that was just 110 years ago today.====JACK: I know why you boldly typed 110. You wanted to correct my 113, without being too obvious..

 FROM FACEBOOK LIZ: I love birds... cockatiel is squawking at this very moment.====JACK; Daughter Beth wants a Great Dane as her next pet...a difference between that and a cockatiel.====LIZ: they are wonderful dogs! i especially like the harlequin. we have a yellow lab, orange tabby, too. all are friends.====JACK: So, if they can get along in the same house, why can't a variety of people get along in the same world? A puzzle.

 FROM JAN IN CALIFORNIA: I'm adding today's "Jacks winning words" to my " special treasures file". It's a big heavy file now but there is always

room for more. Your "words" really touch my heart, Jack. ====JACK:
Longfellow wrote: "I shot an arrow into the air, It fell to earth, I knew
not where..." I feel something like that when I send out Winning Words
each day. Because of your response, I know where one of today's arrows
landed.

FROM TARMART REV: More like a turkey with the distance in mind...but
definitely the start of something to behold then on!====JACK: I don't
think turkeys are mentioned in the Bible, unless it's Judas.

FROM JT IN MINNESOTA: Your message was especially meaningful
today. Tomorrow I am moving David to the Veterans Home. I think it
will be a good move. At least it is my hope that it will be a good move.
But always the unknown is of concern. Your message insprires hope and
faith. Thanks again. ====JACK: Each step that you have taken has been
taken with "care." It'll work out, because God knows and cares about you
and David.

FROM BLAZING OAKS: "His eye is on the sparrow, and I know, He cares
for me!" I had an experience Sunday morning that I termed "divine
intervention, or a quiet miracle" ...I turned a corner on our Lake road,
and smashed into a snowdrift right in the middle of my lane! (our roads
were snowy, blowy and icy, but the highways had been cleared....). I was
stuck solid, a half mile from home in dress clothes and shoes, and no car
or truck in sight. I needed to make coffee, and juice for our social hour,
get to 8:15 Bell choir rehearsal, as we played the prelude, and to choir,
as we performed our cantata during the service! Not to mention teach

adult S.S. class....I tried rocking the car back and forth for 15 minutes, and gained maybe 6 inches. What I needed for the the car to slide SIDEWAYS off of the drift on my lane, and into the opposite lane which was snow packed, but looked "doable". NO luck. Finally I turned off the ignition and just prayed, telling my Heavenly father that I needed to get to church RIGHT NOW, and I needed His help, as I was unable to move, Please move my car! I turned the ignition back on, put it in low gear, and gunned it, and the car slowly moved SIDEWAYS (!) over into the passable lane. HOW, I'll never know, except that His eye IS on me (us)!! I had quite a story to tell when I walked into church! And it all got done, even tho I was a half hour later than I planned to be!====JACK: If I had been in your situation and had gotten free as you did, I would have sung loudly as I drove off...."I sing because I'm happy. I sing because I'm free...."

Monday, December 16, 2013

Jack's Winning Words 12/16/13

"One of the advantages of being disorderly is that one is constantly making exciting discoveries." (A.A. Milne) I cleaned my messy desk yesterday and found some ideas for making Christmas happy and holy. One was to keep a candle on the table and light it before dinner and spend a moment thinking about "the reason for the season." I also found a spike, saved from the track when the railroad ran though our town.   ;-) Jack

FROM HONEST JOHN: My Dad's Feed Store was right next to the RR tracks.   He had a side track that left RR cars with stuff in them.   I loved it out there.   Used to walk along the tracks and find Stuff.".   Built some neat things out of that stuff.====JACK: Kids that I know don't play around railroad tracks anymore. I used to walk to work with a friend, and we'd use the RR tracks as a short cut. We'd see who could walk the furthest on the rails without falling off. BTW, he went on to become a noted economics professor at Michigan State Univ.

 FROM TARMART REV: I remember now, that you have mentioned cleaning out your desk . . . Some years ago I did that to a large drawer in my church office, and discovered a large bundle of mail I was to go through and had forgotten that I placed there after retuning from a vacation . . . a few overdue bills were awaiting my attention . . . 0;-/====JACK: Don't you just hate it when you have to pay a late fee for an overdue bill? Which reminds me that there's a bill in the "pile" for $1.88. The postage and a late fee would be more than the bill.

 FROM GOOD DEBT JON: I found some writing I had begun years ago, related to my current interests. Maybe I'll dig a little deeper today. I like to think I am actually not messy; but just a temporarily overwhelmed neat and orderly person. The truth is, I have been temporarily overwhelmed for about 30 years.====JACK: Sheryl Crow has a song for you..."God Bless This Mess."

 FROM RI IN BOSTON: Every so often there's an item in the newspaper or TV programming under the title, "Where are they now?" That can include stuff we save. Your mention of the railroad spike you saved reminded me that I once had a railroad spike as a keepsake too. I found it while walking the tracks not far from home, and I thought such an odd-size "nail" was unusual enough to save. Now that you brought up your find, I'm thinking about mine, and wondering "where is it now?" Having brought it up, I don't know what it has to do with today's WW, so I think I'll switch to some ideas for making Christmas happy and holy. ====JACK: You and your wife probably have a spike similar to mine. Mel and Barb Rycus gave a plated and etched spike, recovered from the West Bloomfield railroad right-of-way, as a "Thank You" to all who worked on the ARTRAIN project in 1976.

FROM TRIHARDER: or, buy that third pair of olive pants.====JACK: Counsellor....I'm having trouble following your line of thought.====TH: Disorganization (messiness) sometimes causes me to buy something more than once.====JACK: so, you've done that, too?====TH: Funny if you did it on purpose. Add "Ironic" if you didn't -- You sent me the message x 2. ====JACK: Ironic! I liked reading O. Henry stories. ====TH: There are a couple that stand out in my mind: Ransom of Red Chief, and another from which I learned the word "surreptitious" about a man who was "surreptitiously listening to the conversation of two others on a bus -- the conversation between the two was about someone who got away with a serious crime -- but, NO! at the last minute, there was a reversal, as the two men got off the bus and continued their conversation outside of the hearing of the transfixed listener. I don't remember the name.====JACK: One that is popular at this time of the year is The Gift of the Magi.

FROM TAMPA SHIRL: That sounds like a mini version of an advent wreath. You have kept things for a long time. The garage is my challenge for messiness.====JACK: No wreath this year, but we do have an Advent calendar. Long ago, the church gave out dime folders, and members were encouraged to put a dime into a slot for each day of Advent and turn them in on Christmas Eve. Yes, the garage is another messy project for most people.

FROM BLAZING OAKS: Oh, boy,do I hear you on this! In getting out extra bedding in my lower level closet at Thanksgiving, I discovered a box of Christmas vests and sweaters that I couldn't find last year, and KNEW they were SOMEWHERE!! Any drawer, closet, or even my car trunk, not to mention garage shelves, I'm sure would offer up countless "treasures", if given a thorough clean-up! Maybe in 2014...! Hmmmm!====JACK: Now, there's an idea for a New Year's resolution.

FROM BM IN MICHIGAN: Margie would hope that this a good reason for my messy desk at home. ====JACK: Don't you encourage clients to be organized, so that when they come to you, all of the receipts and other data are neatly in order?

FROM OUTHOUSE JUDY: Every once in awhile I will decide to clean out a drawer. The house is always squeaky clean (except when the grandkids are here) but the drawers? I am sure bad about the drawers. I would like to think the kitchen drawers were messy because there are too many "needed utensils". However, we all know we have those utensils we never use but don't get rid of. The bedroom drawers are the same way....well, not all of them but in my night stand I have some sorting to do. ====JACK: Since you're an expert on privies....Did any of them have drawers or shelves? How about kerosene heaters? I know that they had basements.====JUDY: Some of the Alaskan privies have shelves, lights, heater and even bear bars....that is bars to bar the bear from entering. I am on different medicine now and I can use my fingers and hands again! I have read the emails but have been unable to "type" back to anyone. It's nice to be able to be in touch again!

FROM FM IN WISCONSIN: Neat idea for the candle, but what about the spike – maybe you could stick it in a drawer and get it out for Holy Week!====JACK: You don't come across people named, Spike, anymore. The only one I remember is Spike Jones.

FROM LP IN PLYMOUTH: > keep a candle on the table and light it before dinner and spend a moment thinking about "the reason for the season." nice idea. :) also nice to see the positive side of my 'lack of order'... I'm hoping to spend some of my break time to make some 'discoveries.' Ha!====JACK: Don't be surprised if you find something during your search. God has a way of playing "games" sometimes. ====LP: My daughter is Hoping to find my old Girl Scout vest :)

FROM KF IN MICHIGAN: I like finding money in my coat pockets from the previous season , or finding money in the washing machine...money laundering!====JACK: Now, that's funny....and clever, too.

FROM TAMPA SHIRL: Two of the trunks that my Swedish grandparents brought to this country in the early 1800's are still in one of my rooms here. One of my daughters went through one of them the other day and found many treasures including a manger scene that I had bought for my parents when I was in the fifth grade. It is still in great shape. She took it home with her.   I remember buying it at Woolworths in Moline with my money from The Daily Blah which was about the news of our neighborhood and which I delivered at the end of the week. Mother had kept copies of the handwritten newspaper, too. By the way, are you going to have lute fisk and potato sausage Christmas Eve?====JACK: My mother threw my stuff out. But that was after she had warned me, "If you don't clean up your mess, I'm ditching it." Woolworths in Moline...I remember it so well. No lute fisk for me, but I'd like to have some potatis korv.

 FROM CP IN WISCONSIN: I like your idea of lighting a candle to think about "the reasons for the season".====JACK: I like the candle idea, too, but unless you find a candle, put it on the table and light it, it's just an idea. An idea is only good when it's put to use.

 FROM BC IN MICHIGAN: I like this one!====JACK: I think that almost everyone has a messy place somewhere...which means that almost everyone has undiscovered treasures.

Friday, December 13, 2013

Jack's Winning Words 12/13/13

"I am not a person who gives up." (Jen Arnold) I wonder if Jen saw yesterday's quote by Camus, or Ecclesiastes 3. Dr Jen is one of the stars of "The Little Couple" who just received a cancer diagnosis. This comes at a difficult time, since she and her husband have just adopted a 2nd child. Jen's attitude can help any of us when life "happens" unexpectedly. "I won't give up!" When winter happens, I remember summer.   ;-) Jack

FROM KF IN MICHIGAN: Me too!====JACK: It's always happened for me....that summer follows winter, in more ways than one.

FROM FACEBOOK LIZ: i admire that lady so much... sad for her & her family...   :(====JACK: She will approach the situation, first from a physician's point of view, but, ultimately, she's just like you and me. She will face the situation, personally. I have the feeling that she's going to do well.

FROM CWR IN MICHIGAN: Giving up is not an option. Having survived quintuple By-pass Heart surgery, a cancerous Kidney removed and an "undefined" lump in the other one and a Stroke...I can neither complain nor surrender. Neither a "Hayride" nor bellyaching is my lot.....but a beer now and then helps. ====JACK: It sounds as though you could give the doctor (Jen's a doctor) some advice. It might work for her as it has worked for you.

FROM BLAZING OAKS: I was just reading today about this Jen Arnold; apparently her daughter from China has had quite a rough adjustment to their family, as she had never seen "little people" in her orphanage (or wherever she was) even tho she herself had dwarfism, and she was afraid of these small people and cried continually. (Until a "big" person picked her up, or took her!) And Jen felt lousy on top of it! Their little boy Will immediately bonded with them, when they got him, so this has been a challenge. She will give it everything she's got, !and we all hope she can live to raise her children. Drs. day a positive attitude is a great healing help! I think it also helps to keep you healthy!====JACK: Everyone's life is a reality show. It's just that only a few of them are put on TV. Most of us would just as soon keep our ups and downs a private matter. Of course your car problem on the bridge would entertained a lot of folks.

Thursday, December 12, 2013

Jack's Winning Words 12/12/13

"In the depth of winter, I finally learned that within me there lay an invincible summer." (Albert Camus) Camus must have loved reading from Ecclesiastes, "For everything there is a season, to live and to die, etc." In his writings he links the absurd...winter and summer. Life is like that, isn't it? We take the good and the bad, knowing the certainty of change! Don't give up. It's going to get better.   ;-) Jack

 FROM HONEST JOHN: I like the Winter...need, however, only three months of it...then ready for a change.====JACK: Too much of one thing can be tooooo much, except for the grace of God.

 FROM TARMART REV: "Baby! It's gold outside here in Minnesota!" . . . but finally we are getting above zero degrees into the teens . . . not giving up, Jack- "But, Baby! It's gold outside!"====JACK: You know the old saying....Cold hands, warm heart. It got down to 8 degrees in WB last night. That's cold! ====REV: This past week we have been experiencing wind-chills of 20-30 degrees below zero...a heavy coat, hat, gloves and earmuffs were the order of the day.====JACK: You're in trouble when you look out and see people wearing earmuffs while you're preaching.

FROM IKE AT THE MIC: The new phrase about life that I've adopted, "If your life is not horrific, then it's TERRIFIC!"====JACK: Could you be more specific?====IKE: If I could I'd be fantastic!

FROM RI IN BOSTON: That's an eloquent quote from Camus, reminding us hope and faith remain within us. It's like the ashes in a fireplace that appear dead, but within a spark glows that can ignite new fire. When hardship hits hard, we have reason to struggle on.====JACK: That reminds me of a quote that I've heard older men say..."Just because there's snow on the roof doesn't mean that there's no fire in the furnace." I wonder if Camus had gray hair when he wrote those words?====RI: It's unlikely that Camus had gray hair at that writing. As you may know, Camus died in an auto crash at the age of 46.====JACK: Thanks for the clarification. Now, I recall that he dies at a relatively young age.

FROM BBC IN ILLINOIS: One of my favorite quotes and I didn't know it was Camus! He is one of my son's favorite authors. Thanks for your thoughts.====JACK: I'm impressed that a teenager would know about Camus.

FROM PLAIN FOLKS CHESTER: Seasonal changes what makes it interesting. How dull without it. Yer right. Hang in there!====JACK: I'm looking forward to Feb 2nd. For me, Groundhog Day is a sign that spring is just around the corner.

FROM MICHIZONA RAY: I know a delightful woman here who was a part of the French Resistance and after the war would sit with Camus and Sartre talking about their (the French) part in the whole mess that was that war. They would discuss things while drinking coffee at some cafe. I wish I could have been there to hear it...she had such nice things to say about Camus. Maybe this is where the existentialists are so often confused with having such despair and negativity. Quite to the contrary, as we read in Camus' quote...it's truly an honest perspective of both sides of the coin...something like your intention for making the comfortable uncomfortably and the uncomfortable bringing comfort. ====JACK: I can't recall that I ever eavesdropped on some important people talking. But, I have been part of some interesting conversations. Does that count?

FROM FM IN WISCONSIN: Jack, we have had enough winter this year to take care of all of the first three months of 2014 . . . from your choice today you must be having a tough winter too!====JACK: I wear my shoe-spikes when I walk down the driveway to get the mail. No slip-sliding for me during this winter weather

FROM BS IN ENGLAND: I do hope so------it can be quite difficult at times to see the light at the end of the tunnel!====JACK: In the movie, The Blues Brothers, I like the scene where John Belushi dances and yells, "I've seen the light." I guess that was a different kind of light.

 FROM CK IN MICHIGAN: Jack wasn't it the Byrds that said in the sixties a time to laugh a time to cry turn turn turn - to everything there is a season!! So true I find! Maybe they were readers of the bible as we'll! Be good!====JACK: You're right. It was the Byrds, and it's one of my favorite songs. Can you sing it?

To everything - turn, turn, turn

There is a season - turn, turn, turn

And a time for every purpose under heaven

A time to be born, a time to die

A time to plant, a time to reap

A time to kill, a time to heal

A time to laugh, a time to weep

To everything - turn, turn, turn

There is a season - turn, turn, turn

And a time for every purpose under heaven

A time to build up, a time to break down

A time to dance, a time to mourn

A time to cast away stones

A time to gather stones together

To everything - turn, turn, turn

There is a season - turn, turn, turn

And a time for every purpose under heaven

A time of war, a time of peace
A time of love, a time of hate
A time you may embrace
A time to refrain from embracing

To everything - turn, turn, turn
There is a season - turn, turn, turn
And a time for every purpose under heaven

A time to gain, a time to lose
A time to rend, a time to sew
A time to love, a time to hate
A time of peace, I swear it's not too late!
 ====CK: We'll done Jack! That song sure says a lot and offers a lot to think about! I know you get that! ====JACK: I appreciate the abilities of song writers (and hymn writers) who are able to tell a story and set it to music. I think of Stephen Sondheim's, "Send in the Clowns." I remember the first time I heard it. Our church organist was playing it as a prelude. I asked him, "What was that song you were playing as I walked up to the altar?" I laughed when he told me.

 FROM FACEBOOK LIZ: LAL====JACK: I think that means, Like A Lot.

 FROM BLAZING OAKS: I ALWAYS HAD SEVERAL POSTERS ON THE WALL OF MY SCHOOL ROOM, AND THIS SAYING WAS ONE OF THOSE...WITH A

PICTURE OF SNOW ON THE GROUND, AND A SPRING FLOWER JUST POKING ABOVE THE SNOW...YEARS LATER ONE OF MY STUDENTS WROTE THAT THEY COPIED ALL THE SAYING S ON THE POSTERS I PUT UP (AND OFTEN CHANGED) AND THAT THIS SAYING BY CAMUS HAD BEEN HER FAVORITE, AND HAD HELPED HER GET THROUGH SOME TOUGH TIMES! WINTER CAN BE BEAUTIFUL, BUT ALSO STARK AND GRIM. WE ALREADY HAVE WIND CHILL TEMPS BELOW ZERO...TODAY HAD A HIGH OF 24 AND A LOW OF ONE DEGREE LAST NIGHT!
A WHITE CHRISTMAS SEEMS LIKELY!! :-) I LIKE ALL FOUR SEASONS,AND WOULD MISS THEM IF THEY DID NOT OCCUR WITH THEIR CHANGES OF SCENERY AND WEATHER, GOOD OR BAD, CHRISTIANS WILL GET THROUGH IT...====JACK: Teachers can make a lasting impression...and you have been one of those.

Wednesday, December 11, 2013

Jack's Winning Words 12/11/13

"Just move your house!" (Arnold Lobel) Mary, who has a pre-school, introduced me recently to the childrens book, "Ming Lo Moves the Mountain." I checked it out on the net. If you haven't read it, the gist of the story is this. If you're facing a mountain in this life that can't be moved, then look for another way to get rid of the problem. Through the years people have given me personal examples. I'm ready to hear some more. ;-) Jack

FROM PEPPERMINT MARY: so glad to have introduced you to ming lo and co. when we read the book at school, we mimic the closing of eyes and walking backwards. it's quite a sight to see!====JACK: Adults trying to do that might lose their balance and create for themselves a bigger mountain.

FROM TARMART REV: "The Little Red Train Engine"?! "I think I can...I think I can...I think I can..." ====JACK: Not only "I think," but "I know I can." And he did!

FROM MY LAWYER: When mountains can't be moved through a reasonable and respectful process, there's always the judicial system in the United States. Only here can the 'little guy', or David, slay Goliath and be treated on an equal footing in a Court of Law. Due process of law and Equal Protection under the law are the hallmarks of our system of justice. Thank God (and the Constitution) for our system of justice. ====JACK: There may be a mountain of evidence, but with the right attorney, that mountain can become an ant hill.

FROM SHARIN' SHARON: Actually, the mountain in this life has often been the church. I've found that whenever I'm confused about what's going on in my own particular congregation, somehow (and I believe this is God's doing) other people come along outside and, both help me to be patient and wait further on God and many times validate my own hunch/instinct/guidance from the Holy Spirit that my own thinking isn't exactly that far off the wall and I'm not all wrong about things or something. Actually, Martin Luther is a good example to me of a Christian who had to do that too as he looked outside the church for support and nurturing for theological wrestling he was doing too. I identify myself as

Lutheran and in the Church and now not willing to give up on my local Lutheran church when we disagree with positions/stands on various things. It's a much better place to be in than 20 something years ago when I was busy church shopping. That's the personal example that has always been closest to my heart.====JACK: Jesus said, " If you have faith as a grain of mustard seed, you will say to this mountain, Be moved from this place to that; and it will be moved; and nothing will be impossible to you." Can that be possible? "All things are possible to the one who believes."

FROM CK IN MICHIGAN: If you can't move it! Walk around! Too simple?====JACK: Many tough problems have relatively simple solutions, if you give them some thought.

Tuesday, December 10, 2013

Jack's Winning Words 12/10/13

"I'm sad that it's uncool or offensive to talk about environmental or human rights issues." (Grimes) Did you know that Grimes is Clair Bucher, a Canadian musician? Did you know that 20 years ago the U.N. established Dec 10 as Human Rights Day, to encourage nations to improve living conditions for all people? Be uncool and Google: Human Rights Day. See what's being done and how you might give support.   ;-) Jack

FROM DR J IN OHIO: I think the world is changing and it is getting much COOLER to care about the rights of others ;-)====JACK: The deniers are running out of excuses, and their numbers are increasingly smaller.

FROM SHARIN' SHARON: I googled. This is sort of uncool in certain groups of people but I regularly contribute to and am a member of the ACLU which is an organization that, in my opinion, works to give people human rights. Thanks for calling this special day to our attention.====JACK: As is the case with many issues, we tend to be more comfortable with "preaching to the choir." I'm happy for the diversity that is happening in our congregations.

FROM RI IN BOSTON: There is so much about the environment and human rights reported in the media these days, I had no perception that it's offensive or uncool to talk about it. There are plenty of times when people say things about others, or do things to the environment that are offensive, and those are moments when we should speak out against such behavior.====JACK: Yes, there seems to be more in the media on the subject of the environment and human rights, but it's like people listening to preaching in the church. Do they "buy into" what's being said?

FROM TRIHARDER: Gee, we must be very uncool. Very uncool.====JACK: From what I see on your Facebook page, you're not shy about expressing your views on social issues. Cool!

Monday, December 09, 2013

Jack's Winning Words 12/9/13

"Somewhere, something incredible is waiting to be known." (Carl Sagan) I read this week that commercial space flight is expected to begin in a year. Eventually a trip from LA to London will take an hour. Robotic surgery will be commonplace. Stem cell use will help cure incurable diseases. Amazon will use drones to deliver orders to your door. "You ain't seen nuthin' yet." What incredible thing would you like to see?   ;-) Jack

FROM SHARIN' SHARON: Do we have to see drones delivering amazon.com orders to our door? That's a bit too much for me.====JACK: People used to think that it was "too much" when those noisy Model Ts would frighten the horses. But, you're right, a sky filled with drones would not be a beautiful sight, like birds on the wing.

FROM HONEST JOHN: Peace, Justice, and Charity.====JACK: Incredible, but not impossible. As I heard Isaiah's prophecy yesterday in church..."In that day the wolf and the lamb will live together; the leopard will lie down with the baby goat. The calf and the yearling will be safe with the lion, and a little child will lead them all."

FROM TARMART REV: " . . .a "kinder, gentler nation." -George H. W. Bush====JACK: It's too bad that "We ain't seen it yet!" That doesn't that it's not a good idea.====REV: "Somewhere, something incredible is waiting to be known." -- The best is yet to come!!====JACK: As they say in Willmar, "Ya betcha!"

FROM YOOPER BOB: I'd like to see "Peace on Earth."   That would truly be the incredible! ====JACK: One of my favorite Christmas songs is, "I Heard the Bells," written during the Civil War by Henry Wadsworth

Longfellow.

 I Heard the Bells on Christmas Day

Their old familiar carols play,

And wild and sweet the words repeat

Of peace on earth, good will to men.

I thought how, as the day had come,

The belfries of all Christendom

Had rolled along the unbroken song

Of peace on earth, good will to men.

And in despair I bowed my head:

"There is no peace on earth," I said,

"For hate is strong and mocks the song

Of peace on earth, good will to men."

Then pealed the bells more loud and deep:

"God is not dead, nor doth he sleep;

The wrong shall fail, the right prevail,

With peace on earth, good will to men."

Till, ringing singing, on its way,

The world revolved from night to day,

A voice, a chime, a chant sublime,

Of peace on earth, good will to men!

 FROM GOOD DEBT JON: Best Winning Word this week. ...Love

it....====JACK: Sagan was a great teacher of science who looked "positively" at the future. People loved it when he translated science into everyday language. Pastors ought to be able to do that with theology, too.

FROM RI IN BOSTON: This world has become a Pandora's Box, and the rapid progression of "incredible" things coming forth every day, deemed to be improving our lives, will eventually drive us to despair. Like the builders of the Tower of Babel, men believe they are creating heaven on earth, but it may turn out to be hell.====JACK: That's one way of looking at it, but I think that Sagan was more optimistic than that. However, I see that you did quality your answer with a "may." That's always good to do.

====RI: My negativity is due to my belief that most of what is sought in science and industry these days is an effort by someone to make more money, rather than being beneficial to the common good. A lot of that generation of money ends up being detrimental to an enlightened society.====JACK: I wonder if Edison, Bell and Ford has profits in mind while they were inventing? I'd like to think that George Washington Carver did not.====RI: Your point is well taken, but they were of a different era, and their ideas became the means to create more job opportunities. The inventors of television and computers probably didn't have profits in mind either, but the people who "hijacked" those media did recognize the "cuh-ching, cuh-ching" potential and have delivered so much mediocrity that deserves to be stifled, along with the explosion of commercials that smother the media. I know there will always be those who say, "All you have to do is hit the off switch!" however, Sagan's "something incredible" I want to see is the public rising up and shouting "I'm mad as hell and not going to take that anymore."====JACK: Ooooh! You're mad (at something).

FROM IKE AT THE MIC: WISDOM! or how we could all live together in peace..====JACK: I like the song where there's a line..."Let there be peace on earth, and let it begin with me."

FROM WATERFORD JAN: I look eagerly to the future for inventions that improve the health of humanity and the environment. Regarding some predicted inventions--"Just because you can, doesn't mean you should." Right now there are errors being made with robotic-type surgery procedures that a skillful human surgeon could avoid. Air traffic could become a nightmare with delivery drones when there are air traffic near-misses and even collisions happening now. "Think it through before you do!"====JACK Yes, the "what if-s" tend to discourage, but, to me, the major decision is an ethical one...If you can , should you? The what-if-s tend to be worked out in time.

FROM HCC CHUCK: People of the world living in peace, children playing with lions and snakes, God's creations living in a loving relationship..I say Amen to that.====JACK: ...and, then, there is that "peace" that passes understanding...peace, perfect peace. God's peace is beyond what we can image. I long for that kind of peace.

FROM RS IN TEXAS: All those accomplishments and yet man still hasn't figured out how to live with his bother without war and hate. My wish -

world peace and an end to hunger in the world.====JACK: As long as we are who we are, imperfect individuals, peace will have to remain a goal. My next door neighbor and I are at peace with each other. I guess that's where it begins.

FROM TAMPA SHIRL: The most incredible thing for me would be to see peace in the world. I am enjoying the texting and pictures of my grandchildren snowboarding in Fort Worth and of the Confirmation in Ashburn, VA. What an amazing world in which we live.====JACK: The incredible peace that you and so many others long for is the ultimate peace that is found in heaven...which passes understanding. There is relative calm today, compared to the wars we've lived through. But even in our own country, people are at odds with one another over political (and other) issues. Even at that, I like what Yakov Smirnoff says, "What a great country!"

FROM SBP IN FLORIDA: I,too, would like to see and experience world /and local peace.....Which we've been working towards for ....? In the meantime....look what's been discovered, developed, devised , dispersed....and it's all going to advance. Soooo, I would like to see the realization that we can and do travel and expedite life on Mars and the Moon! Think of all the brain power, pioneer spirit, inventiveness, jobs(?)..that would promote!!!! And, unfortunately....conflict! ====JACK: Another vote for peace. Does that simply mean, the absence of conflict...world, national, local, personal? If so, that's why I believe in God's heaven. Meanwhile, my children and grandchildren have had many incredible experiences...but they've never lived the ones that I've had.

No regrets! Maybe, a few (as the song goes).

 FROM AW IN ILLINOIS: This reminds me of a man I knew who was convinced that the windshield wiper was not the best solution to seeing in the rain.   He puzzled for years but never came up with an alternative. He is long gone, but the windshield wiper lives on.====JACK: Do you remember the popular song about the windshield wipe? The beat is to the timing ,of the wiper in the rain.

Friday, December 06, 2013

Jack's Winning Words 12/6/13

"We must realize that the time is always ripe to do the right." (Nelson Mandela) It was said of Mandela when his death was announced yesterday…"He was influential, courageous and profoundly good." He was South Africa's MLK Jr. His birth name, translated, means, "troublemaker." The "trouble" Mandela caused won for him the Nobel Peace Prize. His biography is truly amazing. I liked his smile, too.   ;-) Jack

 FROM CL IN MICHIGAN: Truly one of the giants of our time!!!!!!!!====JACK: I like one of his quotes…"I'm not a messiah. I'm just an ordinary man."

 FROM ANONYMOUS: I heard one man on the "News Hour" PBS say last night that Mandela always had profound "respect for the law." What's so impressive about him and MLK is how these two gentlemen seemed to be able to do what was right and most beneficial to the community, in the face of laws that were not fair and needed to be changed. Truly, a man to be inspired and encouraged by!!!!!!!!

FROM CP IN WISCONSIN: I am watching all the news about Nelson Mandela. What wonderful tributes!====JACK: "Tribute" is an interesting word, originally meaning, "to pay." Now, I see where the word, "contribute" comes from. Many news stories are paying homage to Mandela. Homage is another interesting word.

FROM HONEST JOHN: Isn't it interesting how people like that are hated so much while they live? It seems so difficult to accept goodness in our midst.====JACK: I once had a funeral for an older lady. I did not know her and, so, relied on what her son told me. After the funeral, the son's wife said that her mother-in-law was the opposite of how I had described her. Whose view was the right one? I'll go with the son's. Mandela's words and actions speak for themselves.

FROM RI IN BOSTON: Did you put that second "the" in the quote to see if anyone would catch it? ====JACK: Far be it for me to words into Nelson's mouth, but you're right, the second "the" is mine. It probably goes back to an English writing class. Something is implied. like..."the time is always right to do the right (thing)." You have an eagle's eye.

FROM TARMART REV: He definitely made a name and difference in his world while living!====JACK: Sometimes in death (with the passage of time) people become "larger" than in life.

FROM HY YO SILVER: May God bless this righteous soul in Heaven and protect and grow his achievements on Earth.====JACK: Would that the same could be said about each of us.

====RI: And far be it for me to question your usually astute writing. Have you seen the eye teaser that's a triangle with Paris In The The Spring printed in the triangular space? Typically people don't read that extra "the". Your quote reminded me of that. Regarding Mandela, the real focus of today's WW, he was a global role model.====JACK: I was one of the strange ones who liked English writing classes. I was also interested in diagramming sentences.

FROM BBC IN ILLINOIS: Loved his character and his words. He will be missed, but remain a light in the darkness for all of the lives he touched.====JACK: No one has yet commented on his birth name, which I thought really interesting. It used to be that people named children with descriptive names.

FROM MY LAWYER: After 27 years of tough incarceration, it is amazing that he was able to turn the other cheek. His ability to place his punishment behind him and move forward is one of the great marvels of my lifetime. And, his smile was infectious.====JACK: One of my favorite parts in the New Testament is where St. Paul gives some advice to the Christians in Rome. " Do not be overcome by evil, but overcome evil with good." I would like to think that Mandela was following that advice. In the Old Testament there's this passage..."Vengeance is mine, says, the

Lord. I will repay." . Deuteronomy 32:35   God has ways of working out his will. 27 years would give you ample time to study the Bible and to ponder your relationship to God.

 FROM TAMPA SHIRL: Yes, and it was amazing that he invited some of his guards to his inauguration and that he emphasized that resentment is no excuse for holding a grudge. He and DeClerq together both received the Nobel Peace Prize.====JACK: I hadn't heard that about the guards. I've heard that when people are in captivity for a long period of time, they often become close friends with some who are guarding them.

 FROM PH IN MINNESOTA: try to see the new movie, A Long Walk to Freedom... i believe it was premiering in a theater at the exact time of his death...

Friday, January 31, 2014

Jack's Winning Words 1/31/14

"Sometimes change was good. Sometimes it was exactly what you needed." (Jenny O'Connell) It used to be that you changed oil in your car every 3000 miles. Now, the car's computer tells you when. How do you know it's time for a life change? Every 3 to 5 years is a good time to assess your life's direction. Senator Everett Dirksen was once criticized for changing his mind on an issue. He responded, "The only people who don't change their minds are those in asylums, and those who are in cemeteries."   ;-) Jack

FROM HONEST JOHN: I embrace change.   I sometimes need to think twice so I don't jst change for the sake of changing.   We need some ruts, too.====JACK: You're right! The qualifier is..."sometimes!" My son used to drive down busy Telegraph Rd on his way to work. While other drivers were continually changing lanes, he noticed that if he stayed the course, he and the "changers" would often be side by side at each stop light.

FROM DOCTOR PAUL: Everett Dirksen!!!! Now there is an interesting person that probably anyone under 40 has no idea who he was. I can still here that gravel voice of his. He was so colorful! We need more Senators like him!====JACK: Michigan had some statesmen at senators, too....Vandenberg, Hart and soon-to-be-retired, Carl Levin.====PAUL: Right... And Williams and a republican who could never be endured by his party if he were involved today...Milliken.====JACK: ....and let's not forget about HHH,   Hubert Horatio Humphrey.====PAUL: One of the best and could have changed dramatically from where we are today. That would make an interesting book or movie!!====JACK: I once met him personally...a down-to-earth individual.

FROM TS IN INDIANA: Speaking of cars - Somehow a couple of us here got on the subject of automatic transmissions in cars. Today it is either automatic or manual.   Do you remember the names of the automatic transmissions when they first came out: hydro-matic, powerglide, Fordomatic, Mercomatic, Power-glide.   Do you remember anymore?====JACK: I remember cars that had push-button shifting, instead of gear shift sticks or levers....Chryslers and Cords...there may have been more.

FROM PLAIN FOLKS CHESTER: To change your mind is to admit you were wrong, and that's why so many folks resist it.====JACK: I would put it more positively and say, "I've discovered a better way!" ====PFC: That's because you are not afraid of being wrong.====JACK: As it says in the Bible: "All have sinned (including me) and fallen short of the glory of God."

FROM RI IN BOSTON: Change is inevitable. While it may not please us, such change may be very good for someone else, so it has positive consequences regardless of our indifference. Seems to me we should just embrace change and see where it takes us. It may benefit us in ways that we never imagined. My father when he was a boy had a "bad tomato experience" and he refused to eat tomatoes again. When my mother prepared spaghetti with tomato sauce, my father refused to eat it. After I married and my parents came to visit us, my wife announced she was making spaghetti for dinner, which brought a complaint from my dad. Nevertheless, when dinner was served the main course was spaghetti, but enhanced with butter, sausage and egg...no tomato sauce. One taste and my father was hooked. From that time on he never failed to ask for spaghetti again.====JACK: Did he feel the same way about ketchup? I had a sister-in-law who did not like real maple syrup. She would only eat Log Cabin syrup. Unbeknownst to her....her father would fill the empty Log Cabin container with maple syrup, and she didn't know the difference.

FROM TARMART REV: Consistency is a good practice and one that a person can count on . . . but sometimes change is a necessity because of a better opportunity or because of a circumstance that was not your chosen directive . . . like coming back to you later than usual this morning . . . an early morning notification from the dispatcher at 12:30 am called for some assistance at a home fire where 5 folk made their way out of their burning house . . . two hours later the fire was completely out, the family of five were placed temporarily in two motel rooms by our Salvation Army, and I had an opportunity to minister and direct as a chaplain with the firefighters, ambulance crew and law enforcement on the scene. At my age now, I happily slept in this morning letting the morning fend for itself without me . . . and it did quite nicely I must add.====JACK: I wonder what would happen if, one day, I slept in and didn't send out Winning Words? I would imagine that the world would keep spinning.

FROM TAMPA SHIRL: Life is all about changes and making decisions.====JACK: Every moment seems ro present a fork in the road.

FROM BLAZING OAKS: CHANGES SEEM TO COME FASTER AND FASTER IN THIS HISTORIC TIME TRY GOING BACK TO YOUR OLD HOME TOWN, OR NEIGHBORHOOD, AND IT IS NEARLY UNRECOGNIZABLE! IF WE CAN'T ADAPT TO CHANGE, WE ARE SUNK, EXCEPT FOR OUR UNCHANGING GOD;, THE SAME YESTERDAY, TODAY AND FOREVER!!====JACK: Have you noticed???? When the sand in the top of the hourglass gets close to the end, it seems to run out faster and faster. God's hourglass has an unlimited supply.

FROM DOCTOR JUDY: Really liked this a lot!! Thanks====JACK: As Facebook puts it...LMTA.

Thursday, January 30, 2014

Jack's Winning Words 1/30/14

"The most important ingredient in the formula of success is knowing how to get along with people." (Theodore Roosevelt) Forbes magazine says that success begins when you quit saying, "Tomorrow!" Dr. Phil says, "Find a passion." Paul Getty's advice: "Rise early, work hard, strike oil." But Teddy Roosevelt had the right idea. When you're able to get along with people, "your" world is a better place.   ;-) Jack

FROM HONEST JOHN: I was thinking of you last night.   I have a friend Charlie Bear who sits on our bed who is so much of an optimist that he makes even you appear to be somewhat pessimistic.   I will have to introduce you two some day.====JACK: I used to be a Bear fan, but have switched to the Lion after moving to Detroit

FROM TRIHARDER: success is defined differently, much differently, by different people. And, still, a person may be successful in one part of his/her life; and, yet, a failure at another (or others)====JACK: Just like beauty--success is in the eye of the beholder. But you'll probably agree that "getting along with people" is a positive quality in people, no matter how you define success in their life..====TH: ... and may be defined as a success in and of itself. Some people wake up in the morning have that very goal. ====JACK: ...and some people get up on the wrong side of the bed. Such is life.====TH: Amen Or as the kids say...Your totally right dude====JACK: I was curious. I found out that "dude" traces back to the Doodle in Yankee Doodle Dandy, who stuck a feather in his hat. A kind of foppish character who dressed in a strange way. Doodle became, dude.

 FROM TARMART REV: I try to always remember to "invest in the lives of people" and in "the Word of God" for they are eternal and the only two things I can take with me after death here on earth . . . don't want to be lonely in the kingdom to come.====JACK: I like this passage from the Sermon on the Mount... "Do not store up for yourselves treasures on earth, where moths and vermin destroy, and where thieves break in and steal. But store up for yourselves treasures in heaven, where moths and vermin do not destroy, and where thieves do not break in and steal. For where your treasure is, there your heart will be also." The friends you have are an incorruptible treasure.

 FROM OUTHOUSE JUDY: Theodore Roosevelt is one of my favorite presidents. His advice is excellent. There have been a few people, only a few, I have a really hard time getting along with. Sometimes the best way to deal with those folks are to stay clear. If that's impossible, say as little as possible .====JACK: Teddy also said, "Speak softly and carry a big stick."

 FROM BLAZING OAKS: T.R. is so right. It is absolutely crucial to know how to work, play and interact with people on every level of life! BTW "At Calvary" is a beloved hymn in all the Baptist hymnals... ====JACK: Roosevelt's religious background was Dutch Reformed. He attended Episcopal churches, because that was his wife's religion.

FROM KF IN MICHIGAN: It is a choice, right?====JACK: My first inclination was to answer, Yes! But upon further review, I think the choice is harder for some than others. Those born and raised in poverty, those born in disfunctional homes, those who had inferior educational opportunities. "All are created equal," but not all have equal opportunities. But, choice does play a part. There are those who have chosen to rise above circumstances and have become successful.

Wednesday, January 29, 2014

Jack's Winning Words 1/29/14

"Most people call me, Mercy. I like that." (Mercedes McCambridge) In light of our winter weather, these words by Pope Francis seem appropriate: "A little bit of mercy makes the world less cold and more just." I remember reading The Merchant of Venice as a 9th grader...especially, "The quality of mercy is not strained." And then this truth follows..."Mercy blesses both the one who gives and the one who takes."   ;-) Jack

FROM HONEST JOHN: The OT lesson this week is Micah 6.====JACK: I remember a seminary prof who challenged us to remember Micah's words as we went out to do ministry..."Do justice, love kindness and walk humbly with your God." Martin Marty is part of my generation, and one of his sons is named, Micah.

FROM WATERFORD JAN: If mercy can be defined as kindness given, some of the spontaneous kindnesses I have rendered have brought me exceeding pleasure. They have been pleasant surprises for the receiver and to this giver. Planned mercy through organization programs is also pleasurable--I'm thinking of our church food pantry.====JACK: The Bible passage, "The Lord loves a cheerful giver," has been translated, "The Lord loves the one one who gives hilariously."

FROM BLAZING OAKS: I remember having to memorize that speech on Mercy and recite it to the class, in Miss Garst's speech class. That, and the one from Hamlet, "Is this a dagger I see before me? Come, let me clutch thee!..."   We took it very seriously; I wonder if kids today would?! MERCY, when you don't get what you deserve...or GRACE, when you get what you don't deserve. :-) I lost a much younger bridge buddy and neighbor, early this morning, and am thankful again for a merciful God, when we enter eternity and judgment! "Eye hath not seen, neither has entered into the heart of man, what God has prepared for those who love him"! Mercy!====JACK: I'm reading a book, written by a mother whose 16-yr-old son was killed in an auto accident. Getting what you don't deserve begs for a different word than, grace...or so it seems.

FROM TAMPA SHIRL: We must have had a great teacher to remember that. It was all very impressive. Pope Francis has a lot of good ideas. I do reading his tweets every day, even though my new 5C phone and computer sometimes do mysterious things Thanks for all of the WW. You often jog my memory. ====JACK: Probably, Mrs. Wiggins. I wonder whatever happened to Bessie Mae Coleman?

FROM TARMART REV: There you go again . . . stirring up an old hymn or two:

(v) Years I spent in vanity and pride, Caring not my Lord was crucified, Knowing not it was for me He died On Calvary.

(v) By God's Word at last my sin I learned; Then I trembled at the law I'd spurned, Till my guilty soul imploring turned To Calvary.

(v) Now I've giv'n to Jesus ev'rything, Now I gladly own Him as my King, Now my raptured soul can only sing Of Calvary.

(v) Oh, the love that drew salvation's plan! Oh, the grace that bro't it down to man! Oh, the mighty gulf that God did span At Calvary.

(Chorus) Mercy there was great, and grace was free; Pardon there was multiplied to me; There my burdened soul found liberty, AT CALVARY.

====JACK: I don't think that was in the Lutheran Hymnal. Maybe you can sing a stanza or two when we meet again at Panera.

FROM SBP IN FLORIDA: "Tis mightiest in the mightiest.." Mrs. Wiggins' English class at John Deere Junior High a looongtime ago! "And earthly power doth then show likest God's when mercy seasons justice." I like the words of Pope Francis"A little bit of mercy...less cold and more just". Is it possible for our l our legal system allow for mercy to season justice?====JACK: Sometimes we think that the only learning takes place in college. Not so! I even remember learning about the American Indians in Kindergarten...and also learning how to color.pictures. Jack Kevorkian, who advocated "mercy killing," lived in out community.

FROM PLAIN FOLKS CHESTER: I will be merciful today and not "pull your chain."====JACK: Isn't there a sign at Fejuary Park in Davenport that says, "Don't tease the monkeys?"

Tuesday, January 28, 2014

Jack's Winning Words 1/28/14

"If we had no winter, the spring would not be so pleasant. If we did not sometimes taste adversity, prosperity would not be so welcome." (Ann Bradstreet) We're having the worst winter here in Michigan since 78-79. A friend in the U.P. says that Calumet has had 219" of snow, so far...with more to come. Speaking of coming, I like the Bible promise: "The sufferings of this present time aren't worth comparing with the good things that God has coming for you."   ;-) Jack

FROM TRIHARDER: Is it like knocking one's head against the wall because it feels so good when we stop?====JACK: Strange as it may seem, we may not do it literally, but figuratively is another matter.

FROM HONEST JOHN: With this kind of Winter we should enjoy the Hell out of Spring!====JACK: In the future, when I hear someone complain about the cold, I'll say, "You call this cold? Well, I remember back in January, 2014...That was really cold. This is nothing."

FROM TARMART REV: Well put, Jack!! . . . 38 degrees a couple of Sundays ago, and some folk were walking around without jackets, feeling Spring had sprung!?!?====JACK: Everybody seems to talk about the weather, but we haven't come to the point where we want to do something about changing lifestyles in order to help save the planet. "Go green!"====REV: I would love to see some "green"!====JACK: Are you talking about the offering plate or the planet?====REV: Actually, looking for grass, budding and scenery.====JACK: It's coming, it's coming.

 FROM HR IN MICHIGAN: This is funny that you mention that this is the worst winter since 1978-79. I was speaking to my wife last night at dinner and I said that the last time we had a winter like this was in 1978 when we were in Davenport. She remembered the piles of snow and getting stuck everywhere. Then we talked about the incredible thunder storms we had in the summer. They were tremendous powerful bursts of energy and driving rain, and more intense than anything I Have experienced since.====JACK: I remember something worse that this cold.....when we were without power for 2 weeks because of a spring ice storm. It was cold them, and the sump pump overflowed.

 FROM RI IN BOSTON: I'm not actually thinking a lot about the "good things" that will be coming to me in the hereafter...I'm interested in getting some answers to a lot of questions I have.====JACK: We all have questions, but you and I should try not to be too hard on God, because he really loves us and wants what is best for us.

FROM PEPPERMINT MARY: "the soul would have no rainbow had the eye no tear". it is cold, snowy, and windy for sure...but ahhh...it is so beautifully glittery.====JACK: That's looking on the sunnyside. In fact, that's your song for today...."
Grab your coat and get your hat
Leave your worries on the doorstep

Life can be so sweet

On the sunny side of the street

Can't you hear the pitter-pat

And that happy tune is your step

Life can be complete

On the sunny side of the street

 ====MARY: i'll sing that tune as i walk to school to do some alone work.
we have been closed for two days now and i am getting antsy!====JACK:
How old do children have to be before they can comprehend,
antsy?====MARY: birth?

 FROM DAZ IN COLORADO: There are two people here who very much
believe that.====JACK: ...and it's more than just about the weather,
isn't it?

 FROM TAMPA SHIRL: No doubt the long winter helps to make the spring
so beautiful. By the way, it is predicted to be in the 70s today, but it
will get colder tomorrow (50s) in Florida.====JACK: One thing I like
about a deep snow cover is that it holds moisture that the earth needs
for the grass and the flowers. I'll take the 50s.

FROM DC IN KANSAS: I saw this in KOS --

A picture of Pope Francis with these words:(every other line was larger
print -- so I made it bold face)

The promise was that

when the glass was full, it would overflow

benefiting the poor.

But what happens instead is that when the glass if full

it magically gets bigger

nothing ever comes out for the poor

====JACK: Some people are getting uneasy when the Pope talks about the haves helping the have-nots.

 FROM HY YO SILVER: Amen====JACK: I'm glad that we're on the same page.

 FROM MW IN ILLINOIS: Our front yard is 3 feet deep with snow, glad we don't have to shovel. Saddlebrook is always here early removing the snow, they do a great job. Dick has to get out with his shovel, clears the snow from the porch & deck doors,   this has been the worst here in many years, I'M READY FOR SPRING!!!!====JACK: Winter is a prelude to spring, sort of like life is a preparation for eternal life. One hymn puts it this way: "Earth is but a desert (a snowdrift) drear, heaven is my home.

FROM JK IN CALIFORNIA: Thanks, I needed that***====JACK: Actually, I pray before sending out Winning Words that they might be of help to someone. ====JK: They really help me and I read them every day*****

FROM PLAIN FOLKS CHESTER: LET THE GOOD TIMES ROLL!====JACK: I've seen dogs and kids roll in the snow, but not a grown man.

 FROM FM IN WISCONSIN: A great winning word for a cold cold day – thanks for the word and for your excellent comment!====JACK: I learned that Bible verse from a chaplain who repeated it when he went from bed to bed in Chicago's Cook County Hospital, visiting patients from the infamous Skid Row.

FROM FACEBOOK LIZ: a friend & i were saying how beautiful & bug-free the spring will be! ====JACK: I'm reminded of the poem by Ogden Nash..."God in his wisdom made the fly And then forgot to tell us why." Just as we each have a purpose, I suppose that each bug has a purpose, too. But some bugs bug me.====LIZ: they are a delight on the bird smorgasbord, if nothing else.====JACK: That's a purpose, of course. I suppose a bug might ask, "What is the purpose of humans?"====LIZ: a mosquito knows...====JACK: You're right! We're a part of that "buzzer's" food chain.

 FROM PZ IN MICHIGAN: Thank you for a refreshing perspective on how to view this chilly taste of Mother Nature! It helps!====JACK: This morning at the meeting of the Optimist Club, we heard a mother tell about how she is dealing with the "winter" in her life, the tragic death of her 16 year old son. While the temperature will eventually warm up and the snow will melt, the memory of the winter remains.

 FROM BLAZING OAKS: SO TRUE! TALKING OF BUGS IN ;YOUR BLOG, I HAVE A COLORED SKETCH OF NOAH'S ARK PAINTED ON WOOD IN MY KITCHEN WHICH SAYS, "IF NOAH HAD BEEN TRULY WISE, HE WOULD HAVE SWATTED THOSE TWO FLIES!" AND I SUPPOSE THERE IS SOME REASON FOR THE EXISTENCE OF MOSQUITOES, BUT WHAT??!! :-) ASIDE FROM FOOD FOR THE PURPLE MARTINS.! AH WELL, OUR TIMES OF COLD WINTERS (-7 HERE, SCHOOLS CLOSED, ETC.) AND ADVERSITY CERTAINLY DO MAKE THE

OPPOSITE TIMES SWEETER!! GOOD WW FOR TODAY! IT WAS A DECENT DAY FOR A CWU BOARD MEETING AND PLAYING BRIDGE.====JACK: I happen to believer that the Creator creates for a reason. We can do our second guessing, but until we've walked in his shoes...(Does God wear shoes?) There is so much that is yet for us to understand.====OAKS: ISN'T THAT THE TRUTH...WE ARE NOT GIVEN MUCH IN DETAILS. AS YOUR OLD PROFESSOR SAID, "YOU CANT UNSCREW THE INSCRUTABLE"!~! I OFTEN WISH WE COULD! BUT THAT WOULD TAKE AWAY THE MYSTERY. WE NEED THE 'LARGER" GOD...

FROM DB IN MICHIGAN: Thank you Jack! That is so sweet!====JACK: I remember a basketball player who would call out "sweet" when he sank a long one. Thanks for your sweet response.

Monday, January 27, 2014

Jack's Winning Words 1/27/14

"Criticizing others can protect the ego; respecting others can be educational." (Australian Wisdom) Yesterday was Australia Day "down under." An editorial in one of their newspapers indicates that some of the Aussies (like some Americans) have lost the meaning of respect. I was taught that you respect the flag...and people who do things to improve society. What is it that you and I can do to be more respectful today?   ;-) Jack

FROM TRIHARDER: Yes. Like making fun of others or making jokes at the expense of others. ====JACK: Did you mean to include a "not" in there? ...or not?====TH: "Can protect the ego".;JACK: I was focusing on the last half of the quote. Sometimes in life, we don't consider at the total picture. ====TH: And I was focusing on my own behavior over the years -- Humor that often made fun of others (not behind their backs) -- hopefully not in a malicious way. I hope I never hurt anyone, but I'm quite sure it did sometimes.   Now, it tends to be more self-deprecating humor. ====JACK: I notice that it is often the bane of clever people....seeing something as funny in their own eyes, but not understanding that it might seem "not so funny" to someone else.

 FROM TARMART REV: GIVE THANKS with a grateful heart. Give thanks to the Holy One. Give thanks because He's given Jesus Christ, His Son. And now let the weak say 'I am strong,' Let the poor say 'I am rich,' Because of what the Lord has done for us.   Give thanks.
Someone once told me, "Cheer up for things could be worse . . . so, I did and they were.====JACK: There are soooo many "blessings" that we take for granted. Martin Luther, in his explanation of the 10 Commandments, states the reason for obeying each one of the commandments by saying, "We should fear and love God, so that we....Have no other gods before him." etc.====REV: Good word and thought...take time today to be blessed in yours...in Minnesota this morning, I'm blessed for a heated home!!====JACK: The newspaper today tells of the power cut off for a home with small children because of non-payment of the electric bill. It goes on to describe where help can be found. ====REV: Salvation Army reports doubling of the prescribed budget for heat and electricity this winter...our seven offerings for them during our annual Christmas musical

added $26,000 to the budget needs...they reported $50,000 increase in this Christmas bell-ringing effort . . . I'm assuming it will go fast for additional expense towards shelter and heat. Thankful for God reaching out through various folk to team up and help others in their time of need. ====JACK: This world is a better place because of caring people.

FROM RI IN BOSTON: It seems to me we are more disrespectful when we're in a hurry...rude in conversation, discourteous while driving, curt while shopping...all because we are rushing. I know I'm guilty. Perhaps we would be more respectful of others if we slow down a bit.====JACK: I don't know who it was, but someone said, "I gotta slow down. My feet's movin' too fast."====RI: We'd be better off if we always made sure our brain was working faster than the rest of our body.====JACK: It's like driving a stick-shift. Put brain in gear before letting out the clutch (taking action).

FROM HR IN MICHIGAN: What a timely quote. I have a meeting tonight, respecting others can also twist you up in knots I do my best to follow this advice.====JACK: To gain any respect for yourself, you must, first of all, be respectful of others. Sometimes, easier said than done....but do it, anyway.

FROM PLAIN FOLKS CHESTER: With all of the joshing and "chain-pulling" I do to you, I still respect you.====JACK: Of course, you've seen my disrespectful side, too. Thanks for hanging in there.

FROM BLAZING OAKS: Philosopher Jean de La Bruyere claims "Mockery is often the result of a poverty of wit", but then Ezra Pound, (quoted in the new Yorker) said, "I have not met anyone worth a damn who was not irascible"...So hopefully the witty, ascerbic people will stop short of disrespect, but keep us entertained....I'm amazed at how disrespectful we have gotten to the President of our country, and almost all political leaders, etc. It used to be that high office and leaders were accorded at least outwardly, a certain respect. Treating people, (such as the homeless we deal with,) with respect and some dignity is certainly needed! Many minority people feel a decided lack of respect from most people. We could use a lot of improvement becoming "educated" by respect!====JACK: What I've noticed is how people have come to "demand" respect. I see especially in sports..."He didn't respect me!" There have even been shootings where the "perp" said..."He didn't respect me." Maybe there's a "street" meaning of the word that has passed me by.

 FROM TAMPA SHIRL: Do unto others as you would have them do unto you.====JACK: Ellen DeGeneres often says: " Back attcha." when she wants to return a compliment.

 FROM SBP IN FLORIDA: Respect for..... I'm with those . who say that first one should respect oneself and respecting/loving others will follow.If first we respect ourselves, them we will be more likely to be comfortable respecting others.====JACK: ....which brings us back to, What is respect?

Friday, January 24, 2014

Jack's Winning Words 1/24/14

"Joy, temperance and repose slam the door on the doctor's nose." (Longfellow) Where did you first hear this quote, "All things in moderation!"? Aristotle? Franklin? Twain? Your Mom? I remember it as advice from my doctor. Many of society's ills are related to over-indulgence, be it food, drink, spending. Here's some cutting back advice: List what you really want in life; eat healthy meals; and--take a bubble bath.   ;-) Jack

FROM TARMART REV: ...but don't put bubble bath in a Jacuzzi bathtub . . . the bubbles just keep coming . . . .been there and down that!!====JACK: Some of society's ills might be attributed to spending too much time taking bubble baths.

 FROM JAN IN MICHIGAN: My college roommate used to say, "Everything in moderation, including moderation" (meaning, go a little crazy sometimes). She was the daughter of an Episcopal minister, but I don't know that she got that saying from him. ;-) I think that was just college-kid advice. Of course, now that I have a senior in high school, I'm not quite as fond of that type of college-kid advice.====JACK: When my mother was in her 90s she said, "Now that I'm old I can enjoy eating whatever I please. Please pass the bacon!" One of the things parents can share with their children is a sense of humor. I think that the "moderation of moderation" is a good story to share with your college kid. ====JF: My husband and I are really hoping that Ben chooses Hope College. They start the school year with a "Root-Beer Kegger". ====JACK: They probably have mandatory chapel, too. I remember having it at Augustana, and we heard some pretty good messages, too. But, there's something about "mandatory" that strikes a sour note in our world today.

FROM PW IN MICHIGAN: I can only think of one exception to this maxim, Jack - "Whatever you do, work at it with all your heart as serving the Lord and not men, for it is from the Lord that you receive your reward. You are serving the Lord Christ." (Colossians 3:23-24) No moderation in seeking to serve the Lord in all things!====JACK: Thanks for reminding me that there always seems to be an exception to the rule. Now, go and take your bubble bath!

FROM NO IN MICHIGAN: This one is a keeper! I love so many, but this one really touches my life. Thank you.====JACK: In seminary, we were taught, "In sermons, connect the Bible text with the daily life of the people." I guess it works for Winning Words, too.
FROM HAWKEYE GEORGE: It all seems to come down to PRIDE. Unfortunately I'm guilty of that. ====JACK: Losses have a way of deflating pride. That's why I was pleased to see Alabama and Ohio State lose a couple of football games. God has a way keeping us humble, too.

FROM GOOD DEBT JON: Ah, moderation--the Nirvana of the boring. Moderately successful, moderately at peace, moderately overweight, moderately knowledgeable, politically moderate, can make you moderately interesting to talk to. *All these calls for moderation seem extreme to me.* What great thing was ever accomplished by moderate men or women? For food, though you may be spot on... However I did not lose 57 pounds "moderating" it requires an energy/calorie deficit for a seemingly extreme period of time (660 days for me).   Have a great day Pastor. Love Longfellow, have some of his very old books. ====JACK: Perhaps I was wrong is using "moderation" in place of Longfellow's "temperance." Perhaps it was Prohibition that caused temperance to lose its "style."

 FROM PLAIN FOLKS CHESTER: Use it up. Wear it out. Make it do, Or do without.====JACK: That sounds like a saying from the days of The Great Depression.

 FROM OUTHOUSE JUDY: I laughed when I saw your advice. If I could get into and out of a bathtub I would. This is a saying I heard a lot from all of the doctors I have been to and probably my parents also. Did I heed it? Sometimes!====JACK: You might skip the advice of others, but pay attention to this warning...."Never play leap-frog with a unicorn."

 FROM FACEBOOK LIZ: my mom stressed everything in moderation. good advice that still allows for fun. ====JACK: Good moms usually give good advice.

 FROM BLAZING OAKS: Loved these WW; however Outhouse Judy has a point...for us elderly, it is much easier to step into a hot shower! :-) I think moderation is an excellent word in most cases; in the case of having a rip-roaring good time (sans drugs or alcohol) let the good times roll!! Laugh til you cry, shout and sing! :-) Robert Frost once said, "The middle of the road is where the white line is---and that's the worst place to drive!" Anyway, Longfellow's is a good quote to remember. Thanks! The arctic wind is whining around my eaves, tho temp. is 22...not "moderate" weather here in Illinois!====JACK: I'm looking for moderation in the temperature, but the thermometer continues to stay around the zero mark.

Thursday, January 23, 2014

Jack's Winning Words 1/23/14

"If we continue to develop our technology without wisdom or prudence, our servant may prove to be our executioner." (Omar Bradley) Prudence means, being cautious. 53 years ago, in his farewell speech as President, Eisenhower warned the nation to be cautious about the influence of the military-industrial complex. Wise advice from a former army general. Not being prudent can cause many kinds of problems.   ;-) Jack

FROM HONEST JOHN: Sometimes that military-industrial complex statement is misunderstood Eisenhower meant the military and the in industry that supports the military of course that is exactly what the Reagan revolution is about building up both of those.====JACK: People believe what they think they understand about the Bible and religion, too.

FROM TRIHARDER: The Terminator.====JACK: Do you mean that Ike was warning us about the coming of Arnold Schwarzenegger?====TH: Yes! And HG Wells. And George Orwell and Stanley Kubrick's 2001 Space

Odyssey, The Matrix====JACK: Don't forget the bogeyman.

 FROM OUTHOUSE JUDY: A good example is the IRS and the phone and email messages. That's frightening. I don't have anything to say that would cause national alarms to go off, but this is still a free country. Our whole way of life has changed for the better and for the worst, with cellphones and computers. ====JACK: You were raised in a time when "privy" really meant privy.====JUDY: Well, not really but I did use one all the time at Girl Scout Camp. That was when Girl Scouts learned how to live with nature. Now Girl Scouts learn vocations. It's a lot different. Times change things but not always for the better. I think kids aren't giving enough "Kid Time": just for fun time! It's organized groups now not just someone coming up to the door and yelling "Judy Judy" come out and play.

 FROM SBP IN FLORIDA: An interesting article in this week's The Economist regarding the potentially dire, if relatively temporary, consequences ever-improving, advancing technological advances portend....as job displacement did in the Industrial Revolution and what we witness to virtually every day. Can prudence and wisdom,if they really exist in this arena, stem the tide or....My bet is that we have no choice but to "go with the flow"...and become...====JACK: So, you read the Economist, too? Great magazine! I was interested in the article on the Future of Jobs and a comparison with the Luddites of the Industrial Revolution.

 FROM BM IN MICHIGAN: Like spying on our allies' leaders cell phones?====JACK: I suppose it's necessary to keep some things secret. It happens in many areas of life.   There's a need for a military-industrial complex. Just be cautious. There is a need for secrecy. Just be cautious.

FROM TARMART REV: "Prudence" . . . from the pulpit throughout the pews!!====JACK: Not being prudent in your preaching can be perilous.====REV: A "precious pontificate proclamation!"

FROM PH IN MESA: Read the book Washington Rules by Andrew Basevich (spell?) the military industrial complex that Ike warned about is here, I fear.====JACK: It won't go away, because it means jobs, and congressmen are unwilling to sacrifice jobs in their district for "a cause."

FROM TAMPA SHIRL: If the technology can be used to make a better world, that would be the ideal. It is an amazing world in which we live and must learn to adapt. My OLLI class today was about Nikola Tesla, most of which I don.t understand about AC and DC currency, but his life and work are very interesting.====JACK: I wonder how many people know the significance of the name of the Tesla electric automobile?

Wednesday, January 22, 2014

Jack's Winning Words 1/22/14

"My judicial philosophy is fidelity to the law." (Sonia Sotomayor) This quote came when S.S. was being quizzed about her fitness to be a Supreme Court justice. Is there any quality better for a judge than being faithful to the law? There are other situations, too, where faithfulness is a virtue. In the marketplace, in marriage, in every occasion when we put our trust in people. The USMC slogan is "Semper Fildelis."   ;-) Jack

FROM FACEBOOK LIZ: I like Sonia.====JACK: She comes across as a real person. Each of us is really "real." We just don't always show it.

FROM TARMART REV: Good comment and advice to start my day with, Jack . . . thank you!! ====JACK: West Bloomfield Patch, an internet news provider, calls Jack's Winning Words, "ruminations," whatever that means.

FROM GOOD DEBT JON: IMO, Wisdom and discernment in law are, more than, or at least equally as important as "fidelity in law". That is why we have judges and courts of equity. The equitable thing to do seldom can be adequately delineated by written laws. Where there is wisdom and discernment, I'd presume fidelity would be in abundance. The test is when the fidelity we profess for a set of laws, or a cause is at odds with the crowd, or the money, or the prevailing vision of the currently anointed powers. It is very hard to live a professed fidelity without some common sense and discernment.====JACK: The Law (even the 10 Commandments) is subject to interpretation. So, I guess Sonia's statement can be interpreted, too.

FROM PLAIN FOLKS CHESTER: As a Marine, how can I argue that? I have a Marine buddy who was always being teased by a Navy friend... until he retorted with, "I was going to join the Navy, but then I always would have wondered if I could have made it as a Marine." The razzing stopped. Not the subject of WW today, but a good Marine story.====JACK: As I wrote today's words, I knew that some Semper Fi guy would respond.====PFC: And I was Faithful!====JACK: Just like an old dog.

FROM SHARIN' SHARON: I will always remember one of the people who spoke about Nelson Mandela on one of the News Hour programs, after he died, that Mandela always found "law" to be a pivotal part of a society's working. Even though he was judged and sentenced and served all that time in jail, he still believed somehow that the "law" is a pivotal part of a society's working and never became an anarchist or someone who became finally someone that believed it was the prerogative of the individual to make "law". The person who gives the message can be more powerful when he has suffered like that for his deepest hope and faith and belief in the wisdom of law and actually outlast bad law.====JACK: I've always appreciated Martin Luther's interpretation of the 10 Commandments in his Small Catechism. He explains them, both from negative "You shall not" and the positive, "You shall."

FROM BLAZING OAKS: I admire Judge Sotomayor, and all I've read of her seem to point to a really genuine person. I trust her judgment! I ran across this quote from Abe Lincoln:"I have always found that Mercy bears richer fruits than strict justice." It was in The Wall Street Journal....:-) Which reminds me of the definitions I posted on my computer desk: JUSTICE: When you get what you deserve. MERCY: When you don't get what you deserve. GRACE: When you get what you don't deserve. God's Grace, Greater than all our sin, as the old hymn goes.====JACK: The closest that law comes to grace are the commutation powers given to governors and to the President. When they are used, there are some who complain, because they see it as circumventing punishment. Isn't that what grace is?

 FROM BLAZING OAKS: Profound words for this day and age...Where is Nuclear Power going to take us? It could do so much, used in our domestic lives, but the scary possibility of annihilation due to a careless button pressed, or rash judgment from a nation's leaders is ever present. Our world has gotten so small, due to technology and instant worldwide news that dire situations seem to happen almost daily! Wisdom and Prudence: two good traits to develop and practice, for sure!====JACK: Off the subject, but on the subject...Do you remember sisters, Patience and Prudence, who are famous for singing, "Tonight You Belong To Me"? They're called "the one-hit wonders," because that was their only hit song. Did you ever know anyone named, Prudence or Patience? Faith, Hope and Charity also used to be used as names for girls.

Tuesday, January 21, 2014

Jack's Winning Words 1/21/14

"For me, politeness is the sine qua non of civilization." (Robert A. Heinlein) Another virtue in the Great Virtues book is, politeness. I read that NYC is the politest city in the world. London comes in 15th. Some Canadian police depts are giving out "polite tickets" to courteous motorists. It might be interesting to make note today of common courtesies that you see. What "manners" can you remember being taught in your home?   ;-) Jack

FROM IKE AT THE MIC: Isn't it interesting that if you interchange the letter "t" in polite and the letter "c" in police, then you end up with polite? Could that mean we should police or "ticket" rudeness? mmm .====JACK:. Is honking the car horn a sign of rudeness, or a polite way of pointing out someone else's rudeness?

FROM TARMART REV: "Giving God thanks before eating"; "Respecting adults and authorities"; "Honoring the 10 Commandments"; "Do unto others as you would want to be treated." . . . off the top of my head this early in the morning.====JACK: It's no wonder that you turned out the way you did. When did you become "the little preacher boy?"

FROM HY YO SILVER: Classic

 FROM HR IN MICHIGAN: The author says that politeness alone is not enough. while it is important to be polite you can still be without morals or scruples. He uses as an example the politeness that the nazi guards would exhibit to their prisoners while being escorted to the gas chambers.====JACK: I think that he called them, Polite Bastards. In fact, he used the "B" word frequently throughout the book. I wonder why? ====HR: BTW, I read the NY TIMES review when it was first published in 2001, I think. It received a glowing review. The critic felt that Comte-Sponville did a great job of making philosophy accessible and of writing a book that was good guidance on living a moral life. Easier said...

FROM BFC IN MICHIGAN: What's sine qua non mean?====JACK:
Politeness is "*the essence*" of civilization. There is no cilization without
politeness.

FROM TAMPA SHIRL: If you can't say something nice about someone,
don't say anything at all. ====JACK: There were many like that. A
Swedish one that I heard was "Tyst med du." Be quiet.

FROM FACEBOOK LIZ: i despair if nyc is truly the most polite city. even
chicago is better. ====JACK: I don't trust polls, but like to read them.

FROM BLAZING OAKS: Kindness tops politeness in my book, but of course
a kind person is probably also polite! I'm surprised that that NYC is # 1 in
that category! We were discouraged from demeaning talk about others,
or each other, said grace at meals, were taught to consider others'
feelings etc. in our generation we had no Facebook or Twittering
anonymously. Children were taught to respect authority and their elders.
I wouldn't have dared to sass my parents, as I recall! We used to be more
"polite" didn't we? As a Society, I mean....====JACK: Politeness means
nothing when it comes from an unkind person.
FROM KF IN MICHIGAN: Pretty much I remember manners coming first
beyond all else! Have you perused George Washington's Rules of Civility
& Decent Behaviour? It is interesting and relevant! (I'd be happy to lend
you our copy if you'd like :) Wish I had a few hundred copies to pass
around!

Monday, January 20, 2014

Jack's Winning Words 1/20/14

"Courage is being afraid, but going on anyhow." (Dan Rather) I'm currently reading "A Small Treatise on Great Virtues." One virtue listed is, Courage. No one could deny that it took courage for MLK Jr to lead the Civil Rights Movement....lynchings, beatings, bombings, jail-time. Yet, he pressed on, in spite of danger. Today is not only a time for remembering, but a time for us to courageously stand up for that which is right.   ;-) Jack

FROM TARMART REV: Can even run parallel with being a pastor in a community or world that no longer enjoys having "In God We Trust" life position . . . but pluralistic notions of what life is all about apart from our Jewish//Christian founding tradition. ====JACK: Celebrate the fact that you live in a country where people are free to practice their religious beliefs...whatever they might be. Some people shop at Walmart, some at Target, and some stay home.

FROM SHARIN' SHARON: Glad we have the opportunity to remember and celebrate Martin Luther King, Jr. in our community. In a couple of hours we'll be walking and singing and then hearing some speeches and presentations to help us keep on standing up for that which is right, for the dream that MLK lifted up for all of us.====JACK: A march begins with the first step. And, sometimes, that step involves courage.

FROM PLAIN FOLKS CHESTER: I'd be afraid to jump off the Brooklyn Bridge, and I'll be damned if I'd do it anyhow. Don't mistake courage for stupidity====JACK: As with MLK Jr, courage happens because of a cause. If by jumping off a bridge meant saving a loved one of yours, I think you'd trade stupidity for courage and make the jump. "Greater love has no one than this, than to give his life for a friend (or someone in need)."

FROM FM IN WISCONSIN: What a great word for the day – you should forward it to CBS so that they could include it tonight on the evening news broadcast!====JACK: Just like with some sermons...."That's a great word. I should follow up on that." Sometimes we do. Sometimes we don't. Today, I didn't. Maybe, next time.

FROM BLAZING OAKS: "COURAGE IS BORN AT THE POINT WHERE GOD'S GRACE AND HUMAN EFFORT INTERSECT"...(Father Timothy M. Gallagher) JUST BACK FROM A COUPLE OF WEEKS IN SUNNY CA (YESTERDAY) AND IT TOOK COURAGE TO BRAVE ILLINOIS ARCTIC WEATHER TODAY! :-) BUT A GOOD DAY TO REMEMBER A VERY COURAGEOUS MAN (AND HIS WIFE!) AND ALL HE ACCOMPLISHED WITH HIS LEADERSHIP! WE MARCHED WITH MLK IN CHICAGO, AND IT COULD GET UGLY!! WE'VE COME A LONG WAY, BUT STILL HAVE A LONG WAY TO GO. READING OF MALCOLM BOYD'S BOOK "ARE YOU RUNNING WITH ME JESUS?" IN YOU BLOG, ALSO BROT BACK MEMORIES. GREAT PRAYERS AND INSIGHTS!====JACK: No marching in northern Wisconsin while you were marching in Chicago. In fact, no African-Americans in the community where I lived. We watched on TV. Only later did I come to realize the significance of what was going on.====OAKS: THANKS...I'M SURE THE SOUTHERN MARCHES WERE MUCH WORSE THAN THE NORTHERN EFFORTS! PAUL BICKNELL, A BRETHREN PASTOR IN ELGIN (LATER UNITARIAN) WANTED BILL TO GO TO ONE OF THE SOUTHERN MARCHES, CAN'T RECALL WHICH ONE, BUT WE HAD OUR SMALL SONS, AND I WAS NOT AT ALL ENTHUSED; HE TOLD PAUL, "THANKS BUT I THINK I CAN GET CRUCIFIED RIGHT HERE IN ELGIN!' BILL LED A CRUSADE FOR OPEN HOUSING, PUTTING AN AD IN THE PAPER WITH PEOPLE'S NAMES WHO WOULD SELL THEIR HOMES TO BUYERS OF ANY RACE, AND IN OUR LARGE CHURCH (1176 MEMBERS) HE HAD SEVEN SIGNERS! IT WAS A BITTER BLOW! HE DID HAVE MORE SUCCESS WITH SOME OTHER CHURCHES, BUT THE RESPONSE WAS MINIMAL COMPARED TO THE WHITE POPULATION. THE AD WAS NOTICED, AND WE HAD SOME ANGRY (AND A FEW ENCOURAGING) RESPONSES BY OUR OWN NEIGHBORS. ONE HISPANIC FAMILY MOVED IN NEXT DOOR TO US!====JACK: Elgin or Selma? Really, what's the difference? God is the ultimate judge.

FROM PEPPERMINT MARY: Amen.====JACK: That's a song for you.
 See the little baby, amen
Lyin' in a manger, amen
On christmas morning,
Amen, amen, amen

See him in the temple, amen
Talking with the elders, amen
Who marveled at his wisdom
Amen, amen, amen

See him by the seaside, amen

Talking with the fishermen, amen

Makin' 'em disciples

Amen, amen, amen

Marchin' to Jerusalem, amen

Wavin' palm branches, amen

In pomp and splendor

Amen, amen, amen

See him in the garden, amen

Talkin' with the father, amen

In deepest sorrow

Amen, amen, amen

Led before Pilate, amen

Then they crucified him, amen

But he rose on easter

Amen, amen, amen

Hallelujah!, amen

He died to save us, amen

But he lives forever!

Amen, amen, amen

====MARY: uncanny...i saw the end of lilies of the field today...it's the
seen when sydney and the nuns and, well, me are singing just that song.
synchronicity at it's best!

FROM AW IN ILLINOIS: Jack, when Judy died, I was lost..but then I was inspired to adopt the motto, "smile and keep on going"......and it has helped me.====JACK: I like the words of the song..."Let a smile be your umbrella" when the tears are falling..

 FROM KF IN MICHIGAN: Agreed! A current lesson here would be more courage for students to stand up to bullies = fewer teen suicides! Needs to be taught!

Friday, January 17, 2014

Jack's Winning Words 1/17/14

"I run the race with determination...I am my body's sternest master." (1 Cor 9:26,27) This is the slogan of Team Sweaty Sheep, a group of Kentucky church people who run on Sunday mornings. Their run is followed by a contemporary worship. Their pastor is an actual athletic trainer. A Denver church is named, A House for All Sinners and Saints. What do you think is appropriate when it comes to "church?"   ;-) Jack

 FROM HONEST JOHN: Worship of the Lord.   Can happen in a lot of different ways. Now I have my preferences but they in no way run the gamut.====JACK: Which do you put at the top of the gamut list... Julotta?====JOHN: Nar juldags Morton glimmar.   Jag Vill til stalled ga ====JACK: Here are the lyrics, in case you feel like singing this morning...

 När juldagsmorgon glimmar

Jag vill till stallet gå

Där Gud i nattens timma

Ren vilar upp på strå

Där Gud i nattens timma

Ren vilar upp på strå

Hur god du var som ville

Till jorden komma ned

Nu ej i synd jag spiller

Min barndoms dagar mer

Nu ej i synd jag spiller

Min barndoms dagar mer

Hur Jesu vi behöva

Du käre barnavän

Jag vill ej mer bedröva

Med synder dig igen

Jag vill ej mer bedröva

Med synder dig igen

FROM TARMART REV: The catacombs in Rome sufficed for some of the earlier Christ-followers . . . the front rooms of houses were popular back in "The Jesus Movement" days of the 70's . . . use what we have at the time a place is sought . . . "faithful and trustworthy over a little; I will put you in charge of much. Enter into and share the joy (the delight, the blessedness) which your master enjoys" (Matthew 25:21 Amplified Bible).====JACK: One church that I know of, followed the example of Jesus and worshipped in a synagogue.

FROM HAWKEYE GEORGE: People who worship Jesus Christ as their Lord and Savior.====JACK: Malcolm Boyd wrote a book of contemporary prayers. The title was taken from one of the prayers which began, "Are you running with me, Jesus?"

FROM MY LAWYER: Everything. All inclusive!====JACK: Andre Gide wrote..."Believe those who are seeking the truth. Doubt those who find it."

FROM GOOD DEBT JON: I think "Church" is wherever you are "in sync" and on purpose in your walk with the Creator. This stance isn't received well among many of my Baptist Brethren. I would think God understands and appreciates intent over formal "aisle walking" and parroting an earthly version of what a Lutheran, Baptist, Muslim, or Catholic thinks is "conversion." God must be amused by our antics...   ====JACK: One of the truisms of philosophy or theology is that there are no correct answers, only opinions. Yesterday I attended a meeting held at our local Muslim Unity Center. Their imam is one of the kindest and most gentle persons that I know.

FROM BBC IN ILLINOIS: Appropriate or beneficial or....I think we don't typically spend enough time on praise and worship per se. People seem to either focus more on the teaching, or, dumb it down so that "outsiders are comfortable" which leaves the flock in need of nourishment or stick so close to the traditional liturgy that the insights and gifts of everyone are not used. That is a very good question.   If only we could be open minded enough to allow for different styles/seasons/formats throughout the year.====JACK: Is worship meant to satisfy us, or God? And, what is satisfactory to God? Maybe it's to be private. Jesus said, "But when you pray, go into your room, close the door and pray to your Father, who is unseen. Then your Father, who sees what is done in secret, will reward you." Or, maybe that's taking it too literally.

FROM MOLINER JT: More on "church" tomorrow. Tomorrow is our annual meeting. Although things seem to be going good we need a "shot" of get-up-and-go. Where are the youth?====JACK: Times change, and the Church changes with the times. As far as the youth are concerned, fewer babies are being born, and many who are born are either non-church related or are part of a denomination different than yours.

FROM SBP IN FLORIDA: appropriate" when it comes to "church"? Church can be a building where people gather to be refreshed, reinforced, recommitted, remember, renewed spiritually, while their children are being introduced to the Scripture....all the while participating with fellow Christians/believers. If, however, the building "church" is not a possibility...Must there be walls and a steeple to be a "church"? Do not warm greetings to friends/neighbors/strangers fellow shoppers...praying at meals or special occasions, spontaneous prayers, "Thank you, Lord!" and mini conversations w/God throughout the day constitute "church"???...including our senses during our walks...... For some "church" is the experiences of life, I believe.====JACK: In fact, I once thought of calling my Winning Words "ministry," a *Church Without Walls*, because I consider you and other readers of Jack's Winning Words as members of my congregation. The blog allows feedback on "the sermons," not offered on a Sunday morning. Members of "the church" include people of different denominational beliefs, Christian and non-Christian and non-anything.. I've found, in retirement, a different way to be a pastor, without wearing a clerical collar. My role as chaplain to the Fire Dept, and now to the Police Dept, has expanded the "non-walls" of my church. ====SBP: Just another "I have to." I'm reading Buddhist Boot Camp . Interesting!====JACK: I wonder if that's the same boot camp the Beatles attended?

FROM RI IN BOSTON: What is "church" brings to mind a few choice words..."for where two or three are gathered together in my name, there am I in the midst of them." I remember a worship service you celebrated with a small group, outdoors among the trees of a Lutheran camp in upper Michigan. Very simple, but simply beautiful.====JACK: I remember having a funeral service where one person showed up, besides the funeral director.

Thursday, January 16, 2014

Jack's Winning Words 1/16/14

"You confuse not speaking with not listening." (From the musical, Wicked) I saw a cartoon: "My wife and I had words this morning, but I didn't get to use mine." Often problems at home, at work or in school happen because someone isn't listening. I came across some good ideas on how to be a better listener. Don't interrupt; look for non-verbal cues; repeat what you've heard; seek to understand, not to win.   ;-) Jack

FROM TARMART REV: "Don't interrupt; look for non-verbal cues; repeat what you've heard; seek to understand, not to win." . . . I'm copying and pasting this in my memory this morning in hopes of being able to recall it throughout my day!====JACK: Those of us who, by profession, are public speakers, need to learn how to listen when others are speaking.

FROM SHARIN' SHARON: This is actually an amazing WW. People sometimes "tune out" with each other, especially when they expect the other person or have had a lot of experiences with the other person being "long winded". Remember Archie Bunker with Edith? I hope today I can remember to "seek to understand, not to win." and tomorrow do that again.====JACK: Edith knew how to listen. Archie knew how to talk, but his listening skills could have used an upgrade.

FROM GOOD DEBT JON: I think it is, "Don't confuse "not speaking" with "listening".   Still good advice either way.====JACK: I agree that "your" way seems to make more sense, but I went back and checked several sites. All showed the quote to be as I sent it out.====JON: Thanks. It is a great quote used either way. Life is good...

FROM HCC CHUCK: Great advice!!!!!!!!!!====JACK: Yes, "winning" words.

FROM DP IN MINNESOTA: Great advice!!!====JACK: You're the 2nd person to respond by writing, "Great advice." The other person used 9 exclamation marks, and you only used 3. What do you suppose that means? Probably that the other person needs the advice more than you do. BTW, Mary refers to them as a "bat and ball." Have you heard that expression before?

Wednesday, January 15, 2014

Jack's Winning Words 1/15/14

"One of the hardest decisions you'll ever face in life is choosing whether to walk away or try harder." (Ziad Abelnour – Investment Advisor) There are times when we have to act on the spur of the moment. Shall I walk away from the problem? Shall I face it…and try harder? I'm grateful for a teacher who encouraged me to "try harder." I was "coasting." Sometimes a competitor wins a race simply by trying harder.   ;-) Jack

FROM TARMART REV: I remind myself often to be able to stand someday before our Heavenly Father and be able to say I tried my best in those conflicting times I know in my heart God has purposefully set before me.====JACK: Do you think that God enters into your life as did did with Job…to see how much you can endure?====REV: I do, knowing how much I should endure, giving Him the reigns as I should know to do . . . how's that for a mouth full?====JACK: So he and Satan are testing you, to see what you might do under certain circumstances?

FROM OUTHOUSE JUDY: Great Winning Words! It's so much easier to walk away, and sometimes that's necessary too. But the real challenge is to hang in there if possible.====JACK: To know when to hold 'em and when to fold 'em is important when playing cards, but it's also important in the game of life.

FROM TRIHARDER: When do you cut bait? One more lap, One more try, one more day, one more quarter ..Hoping against odds for success can be a dangerous addiction, too.=====JACK: We each have different levels of tolerance. That's what make winners and losers. Also, some are born competitors and some are not. I think that you have that gene.

FROM PLAIN FOLKS CHESTER: Avis made "We try harder" work very well for them. The only thing you need to walk away from is fear. (Thank you, Franklin)====JACK: The Avis ad was named #2 in the listing of the best top ten ads of all time.

FROM CWR IN WOLVERINE LAKE: ....sometimes,however, the better choice is to 'walk away'........====JACK: You're right. Sometimes reality sets in and trying harder must come to a close.

FROM FACEBOOK LIZ: LAL.====JACK: Hip senior on Facebook.... BYOT: Bring Your Own Teeth. GGPBL: Gotta Go Pacemaker Battery Low.
TTYL: Talk To You Louder.

FROM SBP IN FLORIDA: If "try harder" is done using the same strategy, it might work. However, repeatedly doing the same thing w/no success may be an exercise in futility. Trying a new, different approach/strategy....or taking time to analyze (walking away temporarily) might be beneficial for getting around, through, over the mountain...with God's help! ====JACK: Einstein's words seem to fit. "Insanity: doing the same thing over and over again and expecting different results." But, some people quit after only one try. That's not too smart, either.

Tuesday, January 14, 2014

Jack's Winning Words 1/14/14

"You can't hang out with negative people and expect to live a positive life." (Joel Osteen) Dr. Phil has a list of 15 "parenting" suggestions. A major one...Get to know the friends your child hangs out with. They can be a big influence for good or bad, and the parent should be aware. In fact, even adults can be influenced by the people they hang out with. What is it that you look for in your child's friends...or your's?   ;-) Jack

FROM HONEST JOHN: I think that's where I went astray. My Dad warned me about having kids from Moline as friends but I've had a lots of them. Dr. Phil is probably right on this one.====JACK: I think that the Tri-Cities, Quad-Cities, Quint-Cities should have merged into one metropolitan community, but the voters turned it down. Animosity is hard to get rid of...and so is the fear of BIG government.

 FROM MICHIZONA RAY: Sometimes one cannot avoid being around "negative" people. In these circumstances, one's true "positivity" is at issue. It's easy to become negative oneself about the negativity of another. Regarding friends: I have many friends who seem to serve different parts of my life in accordance with their own temperaments. So, I suppose I have friends for different situations and moods of my own. In the end though, their values, character, integrity, and the like are what are most important for myself, them, and our relationships.====JACK: Martin Luther said this with regard to having evil thoughts, but it relates also to coming in contact with negative people...."You can't stop the birds from flying around your head, but you can stop them from building a nest in your hair."..

.FROM TARMART REV: It's my Lutheran friends who keep me in spiritual shape . . . with Christ's help of course!!====JACK: When God created....he didn't create religious denominations. He is the Father of all.

 FROM TRIHARDER: Perfect! There are people who I consider "toxic" -- always negative. I've tried to limit my contact with them even though they may have been long-term friends. Thanks for crystallizing it. ====JACK: There's a verse in the Christian's New Testament where it says, "So, because you are lukewarm--neither hot nor cold--I am about to spit you out of my mouth." I suppose it could apply to toxic people, too.====TH: I shared your message with a friend of mine. He and I are counseling someone he brought into my life -- a woman (a psychologist, of all things). She looks at everything as a negative. I've been dragged into this thing and suddenly she confides in me for all of her (many, many) problems, most of which she creates on her own by being unable to hold her prolific tongue. His return message to me was that we are such a great help in her life. !!! ??? As Nancy Kerrigan famously said, "Why, me?"====JACK: As a takeoff on Rabbi Hillel, "If not me, who? If not now, when?" Whether someone is an attorney or a pastor, I believe that we can fulfill our reason for being by being available to help the helpless...guarding against becoming part of the problem, instead of becoming part of the solution (if, indeed, there is one).====TH: I'm there for friends. This one is kind of being imposed on me. But, I can't help but help. I know you would and you are a positive influence in my life.

FROM OUTHOUSE JUDY: It's very true. A negative person can really be a downer in your life. It's easy for a person to pull you into the pit if you let them. Our parents were very thorough when it came to our friends...especially the one's of the opposite sex.====JACK: I remember our kids saying (when they were in high school), "Don't worry. We know who to avoid." Sometimes our kids are more discriminating than we give them credit for. There are times when we teach, without knowing that we are teaching.====JUDY: Actions do speak louder than words. Gary's favorite saying is something like this: "Preach the Gospel always and if necessary, use words". That's not quite the way he says it, but you understand.

FROM TAMPA SHIRL: Definitely a positive attitude. Apropos to the subject I received the email I just forwarded to you.====JACK: Oddly enough, your e-mail contains another Winning Word that I will be using tomorrow.

FROM HAWKEYE GEORGE: Very true. Dad stopped me from running with a neighbor kid who later ended up in prison.====JACK: Not long ago my grandson saw a mug-shot in the newspaper of someone arrested for armed robbery. He said to his mom, "I know him. We were in the same class in school."

FROM KF IN MICHIGAN: This has been a constant conversation in our house since preschool. Our tagline was "people judge you by the company you keep"..........in college the message has moved to "lose the people who bring you down" (after trying to help them move toward positive thinking.....)

Monday, January 13, 2014

Jack's Winning Words 1/13/14

"To achieve success, you must 1)Work hard 2) Believe in yourself 3)Work hard." (Poster in St. Leo's Gym) St. Leo's basketball team in Chicago became champions, because they followed the poster's advice. That advice can be a help for anyone who wants to be successful. A friend of mine authored a book of inspirational quotes titled, "Winning Words of Champions." It begins…"God is always #1."   ;-) Jack

 FROM FLORANA NORM: You must have been thinking of me. All very important, but you must have a good plan that can make it all happen. Be able to accept changes and be able to make changes all the time. ====JACK: In the case of the basketball team, they needed a good coach, too. Slogans are just slogans. who was your coach? ====NORM: Lots of older people who I thought were successful. I was also very intuitive and fast learner when watching others. Asked good questions.

FROM TARMART REV: He is in my book as well.====JACK: Most important of all is that you're in his book!

FROM HONEST JOHN: A little bit of talent in your area of pursuit doesn't hurt....====JACK: In his book, *David and Goliath*, Gladwell tells of a coach who took a team of untalented girls and made them into a championship basketball team. I won't tell you how. It's in the book. You can get it at your library. .====JOHN: Overachieving is always possible.   My beating Rod Laver in tennis would have been far beyond what overachieving could have made possible.   Talent is a big part of the puzzle...along with hard work, inner drive, some luck, and other intangibles.====JACK: Gladwell begins his book by saying that David should never have been able to beat Goliath, except.... John could never expect to beat Rod, except...

FROM MICHIZONA RAY: I would add that even though one might work hard, believe in oneself, and perform in accordance with one's plan, it is by Grace that one succeeds. At least this is my experience. I have have had good plans and worked hard, and still lost. I have have had good plans and worked hard, and succeeded. I believe that the aforementioned are requirements; but they do not serve as a formula -- just the minimum of requirements. "Success" can easily become a self-idolatry, and as such, it makes it difficult to get through the eye of the needle. Good fortune is a blessing as much as a fruit of one's labor. ====JACK: The street name for grace is...luck, or getting a break. Whichever term you choose to use, the recipe for success usually includes a number of ingredients. I've had lucky breaks along the way.

FROM IKE AT THE MIC: Like many things in life ,success can not be accomplished with just 2 rules (even God needed 10 commandments not just 2).   In my opinion   #3 Identify your talent   #4 Have a passion for your goal #5 Work smart not just hard As has been wisely said: "Practice doesn't make perfect, only perfect practice makes perfect"====JACK: In fact God's 10 were summarized into 2... Love the Lord with all your heart, and love your neighbor as yourself. ====IKE: I'm sorry to disagree with you, but if we practiced the 10 commandments as they were written of not stealing, killing, etc. We would have a much more civilized society than we do today. Unfortunately the 10 commandments from the bible cannot be summarized they must be followed as is. In fact, the best definition of the word BIBLE is Basic Instructions Before Leaving Earth...====JACK: No real disagreement. Of course the 10 can stand alone. But, as is often the case, we summarize things, not change them, but to clarify them. We are to obey the Commandments because they are from God (we love God and his Law); by keeping the Law, we express love of our neighbor and obedience to God. Not to replace, but to clarify....====IKE: GREAT! isn't it interesting God,Great & Good all start with the same letter?====JACK: So does Google.

 FROM MY FLORIST: Sounds like a copyright infringement. Just kidding.====JACK: You raise an interesting thought. Where in recorded history do we first hear of winning and losing? People before me have referred to Winning Words. I try to differentiate myself by using "Jack's" as a modifier.

 FROM PLAIN FOLKS CHESTER: As Sam Goldwyn said, "The harder I work, the luckier I get." ====JACK: Sam's birth name was Szmuel Gelbfisz. He changed it to Samuel Goldfish and, eventually, to Sam Goldwyn. He's know for his malapropisms which came to be known at Goldwynisms.=====PFC: Joan did a cross-stitch version of this (the Goldwyn quote), which we framed and hung in the office hallway.

Friday, January 10, 2014

Jack's Winning Words 1/10/14

"The art of life lies in a constant readjustment to our surroundings." (Okakura Kakuzo) Did you know that the voice of GPS's Siri is Australian, Karen Jacobsen? She's the one who keeps saying, "Recalculating." Some of us could probably use a personal "Siri" to help us simplify our lives by "recalculating" and setting a new direction. Today's quote is by a Japanese "Siri" who lived a century ago.   ;-) Jack

 FROM HONEST JOHN: I don't know...Siri gets pretty upset if you don't obey her..."Make an immediate U Turn..."====JACK: I was doing a crossword puzzle this morning, and one of the clues was: "In Austrailia her name is Karen." WWs gave me the answer.

 FROM TARMART REV: I had to turn that voice off on my GPS . . . kept reminding me of how miss-directed I am . . . and on top of that, it had to be by a "woman"!!====JACK: Adam and Eve were told that, too...according to those who believe that God is not male.

FROM DOCTOR ERIC: I wish it could change the voice of SIRI to Homer Simpson on my iPhone. My wife is my personal SIRI. She's constantly redirecting me ;)====JACK: Quote from Homer: "Operator!

Give me the number for 911!" ...and you want him to be giving you directions?

FROM IKE AT THE MIC: The power of "RE": RE-calculating, RE-form,RE-gress,RE-solutions .====JACK: Thanks for your RE-sponse.

FROM RI IN BOSTON: Recalculating? "I'm sorry Dave, I'm afraid I can't do that!"   Hal====JACK: So, you're a fan of "2001, A Space Odyssey," too? A really great movie. I can remember where and when I saw it.

FROM MICHIZONA RAY: The comment of recalculation references a fundamental principle in the Bhuddist philosophy regarding the temporality of everything (in this world anyway - a philosophy and not a theology), and their "practice" is to live with the loss of "things", even their own moments. We can learn from this attention to loss, and the appreciation for what we do have while we do have it. For all things there is a season, and a season for all things. We recalculate as the seasons change.====JACK: I've never thought of the idea of RE-incarnation as a kind of RE-calculation. Or, it's like kids playing a game, making a mistake, and calling out, "Do-overs!"

FROM BBC IN ILLINOIS: Yes I have, and my Irish relatives cross themselves all of the time. It's actually kind of a nice gesture when you think of it and take it outside the doors of the sanctuary. They also punctuate sentences with "please God"====JACK: Your response caused me to think....What is it that I do that expresses my belief in God? I remember a humble church member who came to church wearing a suit with a small gold cross in his lapel. I was always impressed by that.====BBC: I wore a cross for years and years, then it seemed pop culture co-opted the symbol, first Madonna, then the rappers. The small lapel pin is a good reminder. Felt the same about WWJD. In the beginning it was a thoughtful reminder then there were so many permutations and misuses that it lost it's power.

FROM TAMPA SHIRL: And isn't that what makes life interesting, exciting, and challenging? Sometimes it is hard, but that is why God gave us a brain and free will to make decisions all of our life. Each day is an adventure and a challenge.====JACK: Confession and asking for forgiveness is a sort of recalculation, isn't it? In the Catholic Church the priest serves as a kind of Siri.

Thursday, January 09, 2014

Jack's Winning Words 1/9/14

"Every accomplishment starts with the decision to try." (Brian Littrell) Which do you think is the most dangerous of the Winter Olympic Games? Some say it's the luge. Free-style snowboarding, with twists and turns, looks scary, too. Life has a way of putting us into frightening situations, some even scarier than the luge. Have you noticed that there are athletes who cross themselves beforehand...and afterward?   ;-) Jack

FROM TRIHARDER: You can't do it until you think about doing it. I agree. I used to say regarding a major "project", "I'm thinking about xxx -- but I won't do it unless I tell people that I'm thinking about doing it."

Often, just telling people about the plan would motivate me to do it. When I was talking about taking my son's soccer team to Cuba, it started with a conversation, then telling/asking people about it. My real motivation occurred when my X said, "You'll never do it." ====JACK: "You'll never do it," is a great motivator for certain competitive people, and I fit into that group...sometimes.

FROM SHARIN' SHARON: I've noticed that there are more people in my congregation who cross themselves during worship now-a-days.====JACK: What do suppose that means? What do you suppose it means to the athlete? I've read that Martin Luther suggested making the sign of the cross in the morning and in the evening. Why do you think he suggested this?

FROM BFC IN MICHIGAN: I think the downhill skiing is the scariest. Remember Franz Klammer? ====JACK: By way of Youtube, you can re-see the Klammer accident. Scary! Yes!====BFC: I don't remember him crashing! I just remember he was so crazy-fast and (seemingly) fearless.

FROM TARMART REV: "Have you noticed that there are athletes who cross themselves beforehand...and afterward?" I love that line, Jack!!====JACK: Have you noticed anyone in an Assembly of God gathering cross themselves? What does that mean to you?====REV: Interesting thought . . . I began doing this when I read some years ago that this was not just a Roman Catholic ritual for other church bodies have used it in their faith expression as well. With that said, you will most likely not (other that on rare occasion as I will be found doing so) see a member of the Assemblies of God doing this. The reason is we have never been led to do so . . . probably as we are found to be on the other side of any liturgical expression . . . perhaps we will regret that someday.

 FROM MY LAWYER: If I were in the Olympics and in the luge, I'd cross myself too, just in case!!! ====JACK: You could be in the Bud Lite TV commercial..."It's only weird, if it doesn't work."

 FROM FACEBOOK LIZ: Like====JACK: K

 FROM RI IN BOSTON: The most difficult part of accomplishing something is to get up out of the chair. ====JACK: I have this saying posted by my computer...GET TOUGH...GET OFF YOUR DUFF.

 FROM OUTHOUSE JUDY: We were discussing the Olympics last night. We have so much respect for people who work so hard to become the best. I can't say I have ever worked as hard on something as they do. We always notice the athletes who cross themselves before and after. It's good so know so many people of all races and colors are connected to God.====JACK: When I was in Luther League there was a group called the PTL, Pocket Testament League. Members would carry a small New Testament with them and pledge to read a verse a day. Is that the same as crossing yourself? : ====JUDY: No, I think they are two different things. To cross oneself I think, is a reminder of Who you serve and you are either asking for assistance and then are thankful afterwards. I don't know why the Catholics cross themselves though. Reading a Bible verse a day is something you to do learn and hold in your heart. Hopefully, then walk in the Light God gave you through His Words. Again, these are just things I believe, I imagine it's different for everyone.

FROM TAMPA SHIRL: They all look dangerous to me. We just have to take one day at a time and to do the best that we can.====JACK: One that I like which doesn't look dangerous is ice dancing.

Wednesday, January 08, 2014

Jack's Winning Words 1/8/14

"After a while, the newness wears off." (Kellie Lee) When do we stop saying, "Happy New Year?" When does the newness of 2014 end? I guess it all depends on the people we will meet and the experiences we will have. I'm anxious for this to be a great year. But, it won't come about by just wishing for it to happen. Some of it takes effort on our part. Hmmm! Isn't that the way it is with relationships, too.   ;-) Jack

FROM MICHIZONA RAY: I have clothes that I bought in 1994, and now have holes worn right through the fabric. I know I have to give them up....but I don't want to. They have become so very comfortable with age. I suppose relationships can be like this too, if we wear them well!====JACK: There's an expression that's seldom heard anymore...referring to someone as "an old shoe," meaning...I'm comfortable with that person. A couple of old shoes that I know recently celebrated their 60th wedding anniversary.

FROM TARMART REV: Another fine word for us to contemplate, Jack . . .

off to Fargo, ND right now to talk to a group of pastors, hoping to stir one or two to consider representing Railroad Chaplains of America in that region so I won't have to always drive those 3-4 hours over there doing the same. "It won't just happen . . . it takes an effort on someone's heart to make it known."====JACK: Rather than "it takes an effort," I think it takes a sense of "being called by God," to do his ministry. I like this poem which says it well:

Christ has no hands but our hands to do His work today

He has no feet but our feet to lead men in the way

He has no tongue but our tongue to tell men how He died

He has no help but our help to bring them to His side.

We are the only Bible the careless world will read,

We are the sinner's gospel; we are the scoffer's creed;

We are the Lord's last message, given in word and deed;

What if the type is crooked? What if the print is blurred?

What if our hands are busy with other work than His?

What if our feet are walking where sin's allurement is?

What if our tongue is speaking of things His lips would spurn?

How can we hope to help Him or welcome His return?

—Annie Johnston Flint

 FROM IKE AT THE MIC: I find it interesting that everyone feels obligated to make resolutions on New Year's day, loosely defined "re" from the Latin is try again & then of course we're left with the rest of the word being solutions.. So... on January 1st we should wish each other a HAPPY NEW YEAR; thereafter, we should wish each other HAPPY RESOLUTION!...mmmm====JACK: I like your suggestion to call them New

Year re-solutions!

FROM AW IN MICHIGAN: Happy New Year, Jack. You are off to a great start with Winning Words in 2014.====JACK: There was a time when the school day began with students singing to the teacher...
"Good morning to you, good morning to you, we're all in our places with bright shining faces. What a wonderful way to start a new day." Winning Words is a good way for me to start a new day. I'm glad that you enjoy them.

FROM PRDM IN MICHIGAN: Well written...Thanks! ...and Happy New Year.====JACK As the old song goes...If you're happy and you know it, say AMEN..

FROM OUTHOUSE JUDY: This will be a great year...they all are. Everyone suffers from something...ill health, lack of funds, low paying jobs...etc. But each day we wake up to a new beginning. How we deal with our new beginnings each day is up to each of us. My parents seemed so excited by the new day each day. My dad would holler up the stairs to us girls still sleeping "Wake up, it's daylight in the swamp!" Sometimes I liked to hear him yell it and sometimes not so much. I would love to hear it one more time from him now. I bet the angels wake up to him hollering everyday!====JACK: We each have triggers that activate our memories. "Wake up, it's daylight in the swamp," is certainly a special one. In my imagination, I can hear it now.

FROM DB IN MICHIGAN: Hi Jack, I have a burning question.........You mentioned relationships. How does one avoid "buyer's remorse"? (how does one know when a person is right for them) How does one find the right person? Should they create a long check-list of questions?====JACK: There's not a "one size fits all" answer to your question. I like the expression, "Fall in love, head first." I had reservations about one of the first marriages that I performed. It lasted over 50 years. One that I was "sure" about lasted only two weeks.

FROM GOOD DEBT JON: January 15th, officially.====JACK: Does the same "official" have an opinion as to the date when we should stop saying, "Merry Christmas?"

FROM TRIHARDER: I remember when the love of my life arrived in Detroit. I couldn't wait to get home -- even though some work nights were very long. I called her "my new toy". Less than a year later, we were married. 21 years later, divorced. Yes, the newness wears off. Sometimes, though, the patina enhances the newness. Sometimes, it's rust.====JACK: Things happen. I loved my 55 red and cream Chevy Bel-Air hardtop. I traded her in for a 57 Ford, which was lemon. I keep a model of the Bel-Air by my computer, remembering the good old days.====TH: I had a Rocket 88 Olds convertible, white, with a 400 cu in engine. I don't know why I ever got rid of it. It was reliable, smooth and fast. I could nurse about 20 mpg out of it if I drove carefully -- which I usually did. My first car was a red Plymouth Valiant convertible with a "white" top (that was gray by the time that I inherited it -- from my brother -- who got it from our mother. Push button transmission.====JACK: My Uncle John always drove Oldsmobiles. As a teen-ager, I remember going with him to the Olds dealer when he picked out a new silver Rocket 88. What a beautiful automoble!

FROM PLAIN FOLKS CHESTER: Just because it isn't new, doesn't mean it is old. Some things are timeless. Like the day my daughter was born. Seems like only yesterday.====JACK: When our first daughter was born, fathers were not permitted in the delivery room. After a long period of time, I went up to the nurses' station to ask about how things were going. Oh, your daughter was born a couple of hours ago. I guess they forgot to tell you.

FROM DAZ IN COLORADO: Its been 54 days and its still new. (and great)====JACK: As long as you're counting, you might want to read the words by Elizabeth Barrett Browning...."How do I love thee? Let me count the ways. I love thee to the depth and breadth and height My soul can reach, etc."

FROM SBP IN FLORIDA: Haven't really thought about how the 2014's "newness wears off"...."til today's WW. For me, I guess, it's like "This is the first day of the rest of your life." And, actually, this moment is the first of the rest of my life. But/and we/I just keep on keepin on....moment to moment. ."It's daylight in the swamp!"....is part of my childhood memory bank. Along with lumberjack tales and copper mining experiences.....and pasties. Awesome!====JACK: I'd almost forgotten about your U.P. roots. A friend of mine who lives in Calumet says that they've had over 140 inches of snow so far. BTW, speaking of "keeping on," there's an old Swedish hymn that I like..

Day by day, your mercies, Lord, attend me, bringing comfort to my anxious soul.

Day by day, the blessings, Lord, you send me draw me nearer to my heav'nly goal.

Love divine, beyond all mortal measure, brings to naught the burdens of my quest;

Savior, lead me to the home I treasure, where at last I'll find eternal rest.

Day by day, I know you will provide me strength to serve and wisdom to obey;

I will seek your loving will to guide me o'er the paths I struggle day by day.

I will fear no evil of the morrow, I will trust in your enduring grace.

Savior, help me bear life's pain and sorrow till in glory I behold your face.

Oh, what joy to know that you are near me when my burdens grow too great to bear;

oh, what joy to know that you will hear me when I come, O Lord, to you in prayer.

Day by day, no matter what betide me, you will hold me ever in your hand.

Savior, with your presence here to guide me, I will reach at last the promised land.

Tuesday, January 07, 2014

Jack's Winning Words 1/7/14

"A pound of pluck is worth a ton of luck." (James A. Garfield) There was a Garfield School in the city where I grew up. I only knew that Garfield was a U S President. But, now, this quote interests me. "Pluck" means, continuing to do something, in spite of difficulty. Our 20th Pres also said: "I've had many troubles, but the worst of them never came." Somebody had a good idea when they named that school, Garfield.   ;-) Jack

FROM HONEST JOHN: I remember driving home from the Heart of America Debate Tourney in Kansas...horrible snowstorm....had to get out and put chains on my tires...not easy to do in a snowstorm ...wearing a suit...put pjs on over my unit ....made it back to Augie.   Prof Holcomb was confident all the way...I was not as confident....more like terrified====JACK: A good example of Pluck!

FROM TARMART REV: We have one in Willmar, MN too . . . it was closed when the town consolidated two of the old grade schools into a new facility . . . the Garfield building now is at the present "a pound of pluck" as it is used strictly for specialized educational activities.=====JACK: A church building is a building. What's important is what is going on inside. The same can be said of the Garfield building..

FROM SHARIN' SHARON: I remember coming back from Texas, my daughter was driving, just after Katrina hit--we hadn't realized there would be a big swath of rain all up and down the country. It was pouring down, for miles and miles so that all we could follow were the taillights in front of us. Brenda driving, me sitting white-knuckled beside her, both of us praying. Glad to get through that time!!!!! ====JACK: I had a similar experience in a snowstorm. We had to follow the taillights of a semi. When he pulled off at at exit, prayer took over.

FROM RI IN BOSTON: Regarding Garfield's troubles, the "worst of them" did come, when he was assassinated after just a few months into his presidency. I remember when I was in elementary school, and beginning to study American history, I was dumbfounded to find that anyone would kill a President. But we live and learn. It's clear that radicals have pluck too.====JACK: After reading more about Garfield, it's clear that his legacy was more than his 200-day presidency. How would you or I like to be remembered only for 200 days out of our lifetime?====RI: Garfield did have a record of accomplishments in the House of Representatives prior to his election to the Presidency. He showed plenty of personal pluck, from his humble life on the farm to statesman. He has been the only sitting Representative that ever got elected President.

FROM DAZ IN COLORADO: Garfield was a Civil War General and on Gen Rosecrans staff at the battle of Chickamauga in Sept 1863. Rosecrans was fired after the battle which the Union lost..====JACK: Another chapter in "the rest of the (Garfield) story." We each have our "untold" stories that people haven't heard.

FROM JE IN MICHIGAN: Happy 2014. I really like today's quote as it reminds me to spend time being proactive, not worrying. I like Garfield's second quote also.====JACK: In fact, there's a whole slew (when have you used that word?) of good Garfield quotes. I think that we could do a better job of naming schools these days...using the name as a teaching tool.

 FROM GOOD DEBT JON: I used to remember the word "pluck or plucky" by thinking of the "p" as representing "problems" that you work through to get to the remainder "luck." p-lucky, if you work through your problems you'll create luck. Others say luck is when "preparation meets opportunity." So the p in plucky could be for preparation, or even perseverance. I suppose you could be plucky in love too. It's a bit of an archaic word, but , I like it.====JACK: Lake Superior State Univ annually makes a list of words that should be dropped from usage (like, selfie). Someone should make a list of words that are worth rediscovering from the past...like the word, pluck.====JON: Great idea; I tried BringItBack.com and there is a site for that. I'll see if I now anyone that has experience with Wiki's the idea would be best policed and produced by users and those that love language and learning. Time to maintain a site would be the problem. I love the idea but it is time intensive.====JON: I had an Oak on my land once, that the tree guy said was 350 years old. I have 40 to 43 years left probably (I presume I will live to be 100). I need to figure out the best way I can leave a positive legacy using fast growing bambo and pine....   In my youth often I was too busy cutting trees without planting their replacements....

FROM FACEBOOK LIZ: I live near Garfield!====JACK: I take it that you mean, the school. President Garfield is now in a cemetery in Cleveland, Ohio.

FROM DMF IN MINNESOTA: It looks like Garfield School is still in operation…..but maybe not for long. The Moline School Board has voted to close it. Garfield, situated in a residential area bordering a small business district, opened its doors in 1901 and presently serves 330 students. Garfield Elementary School has long established itself as a viable force in striving for excellence in education.====JACK: Five of the schools I attended in Moline are no longer in existence, but they still exist in my memory bank.

FROM PH IN MESA: was he any relation to Garfield, the cat?====JACK: The cat has nine lives. James Garfield had only one…cut short by an assassin's bullet.

FROM OUTHOUSE JUDY: These quotes hit the mark. I especially like the last one. Garfield must have had a lot of troubles just being President. I wonder if the cartoon Garfield was created to emulate the president. Garfield the cat definitely had plunk. It was Andy's favorite cartoon character.====JACK: The cartoon cat was named after the cartoonist's grandfather.

FROM MOLINER JT: Garfield is closing in 2 years. Rebuilding Hamilton into a modern day grade school. Never went to Garfield but I'll miss it.====JACK: Garfield was modern in its heyday. BTW, what's a heyday?

FROM YOOPER BOB: In 1932 the Finnish Bethlehem Church burnt. Rather than rebuild they purchased the GARFIELD school and playground. They remodeled it which following the mergers became Faith Lutheran. The playground area is why Faith is the only congregation in Calumet with a parking lot! ====JACK: I suppose that most of the year it's used as a hockey rink.

FROM RJP IN NAPLES: And I grew up playing in Garfield Park on the west side of Chicago. Sure wish kids today were given a better sense of history.====JACK: Every generation's sense of history is different than the previous one's. I confess that I didn't know much about Garfield until I researched his quote. The kids of today have history at their "fingertips," instead reading it in books, like I did...for better or worse..

Friday, February 28, 2014

Jack's Winning Words 2/28/14

"We know what we are, but know not what we may be."
(Shakespeare) Did you have a dream of what you wanted to be when you grew up? I wanted to be a fireman and never thought of becoming a pastor. Life has interesting twists and turns, doesn't it? I believe in "free will," but I also believe that God gives a nudge now and then. Today, we are where we are! About tomorrow,...Doris Day sang, "Que sera, sera."   ;-) Jack

FROM MICHIZONA RAY: Life (our time on earth) seems to be a huge crucible that holds everyone, molding and refining each one of us into the gold we are. Maybe this is why our latter days are called the golden years.===JACK: Let's hope it's not "old" fool's gold.

FROM HONEST JOHN: I wanted to run my Dad's Feed Store and/or be a farmer....so gardening has become an avocation.====JACK: Actually, instead of becoming a seller of the seed, you followed the parable and became a sower of the seed.====JOHN: And, a Caregiver to the growing plants...still do that in the garden.====JACK: You're right. It's one thing to sow the seed, but to be a true farmer (pastor) the plants that come up need to be cared for.

FROM TARMART REV: The best is yet to come for both of us, Jack! Maybe tomorrow, if God wills!! ====JACK: That's the optimistic way to look at the future.

FROM IKE AT THE MIC: You're a GREAT pastor!   With your personality & wisdom I'm sure you've subdued many "fire storm" marriage relationships.====JACK: Whatever good comes from my ministry is because of the power and grace of God. I'm reminded of this song....
My God and I will go for aye together,
We'll walk and talk as good friends should and do;
This earth will pass, and with it common trifles,
But God and I will go unendingly;
This earth will pass, and with it common trifles,
But God and I will go unendingly.

FROM HUNGRY HOWIE: So thus the chaplain role, see how things somehow work out=====JACK: One of the sentences I often use when talking with people (after praying with them) is, "It'll work out," and it usually does.

FROM PLAIN FOLKS CHESTER: You became a fireman after all. You save people.====JACK: God does the saving; I simply try to raise the ladder.====PFC: That still makes you a fireman.

FROM OUTHOUSE JUDY: I wanted to be a forest ranger but there were no woman allowed at the time. So I became a legal secretary. How times have changed!====JACK: Yes, times have changed. Now, you could even be a pastor, head of General Motors, or maybe President of the United States.

FROM DS IN SAN DIEGO: Jack, I'm still wondering what God has in mind for me. I'm still "here" for some reason....I really believe that. You and my brother Roland (now Paul Roland) I believe are about the same age....you probably knew him. . FROM DS IN SAN DIEGO: Jack, I'm still wondering what God has in mind for me. I'm still "here" for some reason....I really believe that. You and my brother Roland (now Paul Roland) I believe are about the same age....you probably knew him. FROM DS IN SAN DIEGO: Jack, I'm still wondering what God has in mind for me. I'm still "here" for some reason....I really believe that. You and my brother Roland (now Paul Roland) I believe are about the same age....you probably knew him. He has been in an alzheimer's care facility for the last year or so. I still talk to him and I try to bring up things he might recall from the "old days". He actually looks good, but boy, what the mind can do for you. I hope the good Lord doesn't have that in store for me. He has been in an alzheimer's care facility for the last year or so. I still talk to him and I try to bring up things he might recall from the "old days". He actually looks good, but boy, what the mind can do for you. I hope the good Lord doesn't have that in store for me.

He has been in an alzheimer's care facility for the last year or so. I still talk to him and I try to bring up things

he might recall from the "old days". He actually looks good, but boy, what the mind can do for you. I hope the good Lord doesn't have that in store for me.=====JACK: I'm sorry to hear about your brother.   I'll be offering a prayer for him today. We don't what's in store from one day to the next. All we can do is put our trust in God's grace. One of the hymns we used to sing at Trinity-Moline has brought me comfort. Perhaps it will relate to you.   OUR TIMES ARE IN THY HAND   - William F. Lloyd (adapted)-

Our times are in Thy hand; Father, we wish them there;

Our life, our souls, our all we leave Entirely to Thy care.

Our times are in Thy hand, Whatever they may be;

Pleasing or painful, dark or bright; As best they seem to Thee.

Our times are in Thy hand; Why should we doubt or fear?

Our Father's hand will never cause His child a needless tear.

Our times are in Thy hand, O Lord, our Advocate!

Nor is that hand outstretched in vain, For us to supplicate.

Our times are in Thy hand; We'll always trust in Thee.

Till we have left this weary land, And all Thy glory see.

 ====DS: If God has a face, I'll bet he smiles when he sees how people like you appreciate his blessings..

FROM WISCONSIN JEANNE: I am so blessed. From the time I was a little girl I wanted to be a wife, mommy, and teacher. I am and have been all those things and then God REALLY blessed me with something I had not even thought of when I was young - GRANDCHILDREN!====JACK: If God has a face, I'll bet he smiles when he sees how people like you appreciate his blessings..

FROM BLAZING OAKS: Reminds me of the plaque I have with "Please be patient...God is not finished with me yet!" We are "becoming" until we leave this Earth, but in the 8th decade, one feels pretty well "completed"! I wanted to be a teacher, which I didn't acccomplish until I was 40, but enjoyed my 24 yrs at it! Most girls in our generation wanted to be wives and mothers, (grandmothers!) which is still the most satisfying thing in my life. But the plus of world travel, a career, participation in sports and acting/singing etc. sure filled the cup "over the top!" I hadn't planned to be a pastor's wife but God had other ideas!! HA! Blessings abound!====JACK: I remember the story of a woman who had many medical problems. She was continually in and out of the hospital, but always had a cheerful disposition. During her hospital stays she had a way of passing that positive attitude on to others. Once, when she was registering again as a patient, she was heard to say, "I wonder what God has for me to do this time?" That reminds me of Hubert Humphrey. When he was in the hospital for the cancer that would ultimately take his life, he would be found going up and down the halls, greeting other patients and cheering them up. What a fine man!

Thursday, February 27, 2014

Jack's Winning Words 2/27/14

"Home is where our feet may leave, but not our hearts." (Oliver Wendell Holmes) What's wrong? I Googled "There's no place like home" and got a Motley Crue song. I expected Dorothy and the Wizard of Oz. In life, many of us follow yellow brick roads and leave home in the rearview mirror. The wrecking ball destroyed my home in Moline, but it didn't destroy my memories. Do you have a "no place like" memory?   ;-) Jack

FROM TARMART REV: Living it as we correspond today, Jack . . . I've found it took many other "feeling at home" experiences before I discovered this one over twenty years ago.====JACK: You have a unique ministry. It's not for everyone, but that why you do it so well...and the popcorn is a side benefit.

FROM PEPPERMINT MARY: i don't have to think back very far. i experience "no place like home" everyday when i step through the door, no matter which of the eight homes i've lived in my life. i love home. ====JACK: I read recently that "Home is where the pillow fits your head." Ahhhh!====MARY: exactly!

FROM TRIHARDER: I've recently befriended two guys who I went to high school with in Oak Park. I was never close with either. Peripherally friendly with one of the guys; not even a word to the other all through high school. The first is a "mad" scientist in SF; the second of the two is a photographer (not wedding) in Israel. The three of us lived in the same

neighborhood in Detroit (near NW side), the Dexter/Joy Road/Davison neighborhood, a Jewish area in the mid 50s, it rapidly changed and became a "black" neighborhood. We all took a photo trip down memory land courtesy of Google Maps and made a real connection as friends through the pictures of google, each of us locating our homes and talking about the businesses that didn't survive -- the Dexter Theater, Dexter Chevrolet, the Grand River Theater, Velvet Peanut Butter, ... Quite a connection for the three of us. ====JACK: One of the benefits of the internet is that it allows us to "go home again" and reconnect with people who otherwise would be lost in the dust of the passing parade.====TH: In many cases for me, very meaningful people.====JACK: Most people have "meaning" when you get to know them.====TH: Some have the wrong meaning. Fortunately most do.
Present company included.====JACK: Wrong or right, the outcome is usually positive, when we seek to understand "the meaning" in the people we meet up with.

 FROM RI IN BOSTON: On a sentimental journey there are a lot of stopping places. They are milestones of different sorts, but almost all seem to be linked to "home". Experiences like sliding down the straw stack in the field, swimming in the pond in the meadow, and eating a fresh juicy peach right off the tree in the orchard. In later years, going back to the home where I grew up, I found special satisfaction sitting in the shade of several tall trees that I planted as a kid, when they were hardly more than twigs. There are proud memories like coming up our driveway in the first jalopy I bought, or driving out the driveway of my girlfriend's home on our first date. There's a list of homes we've had since then, and each one has its own set of treasured memories.====JACK: Back in the 70s, Mary transplanted, into our front yard, a twig of a tree from from the property where our church was being built. It had a thin double trunk, until you pruned it. Mary held her breath. Now, it is a stately one-trunk beautiful maple shade tree. Thank you!====RI: That's the sort of thing I enjoy recounting. Thanks for remembering and telling me about it. On another note, I like comments of yours such as "made a withdrawal from my memory bank."

FROM QUILTING CAROL IN RICE LAKE: Our Lake Villa home is no longer standing, but like you we all have our happy memories of living there. I'm sure the school now owns the property. The mighty oaks are still standing.====JACK: I drove by that LV property a few months ago and made a withdrawal from my memory bank. Those were good old days.

FROM HONEST JOHN: My folks built our house the year before I was born it was on 11 acres I absolutely loved it there.====JACK: Didn't you once tell me that you had room for a big garden on that property? Those were the days when people grew a lot of their food. Why don't we do that anymore? ====JOHN: We had a vineyard, fruit trees, berries...it was a paradise for me.====JACK: Was there also a serpent?

FROM HCC CHUCK: WOW, I have many, Grandpa Cobb's old homestead still stands and is occupied by a cousin, the home I grew up in still stands but is owned by someone I do not know, we have lived in six homes in NY and Mich all still stand and hold many fond memories, one is lived in by our youngest daughter ====JACK: A few months ago daughter Beth and I stood in the street looking at the house in Grayslake where she lived as a child. We didn't know the people living there now, but a young girl came out and asked if she could help us. After explaining what we were doing, she invited us in to look around. She had lived in that house all her life and was excited to meet someone who had grown up in there, also. Maybe you can have a similar experience. Just go and stand in the street, gawking!.====CHUCK: Have done that and usually if someone is at home you get invited in for a tour Great help with memories

FROM OUTHOUSE JUDY: My yes, we do have some very special memories of homes we have lived in or had loved ones who lived there. When you leave someplace you love, you leave a little part of yourselves there too. ====JACK: Is the outhouse still standing out in the back?

FROM GOOD DEBT JON: As Samuel Smiles said in Home, "If they have enjoyed the advantage of neither the home nor school, but have been allowed to grow up untrained, untaught, and undisciplined, then woe to themselves—woe to the society of which they form part." Maybe what we learn at "home" is just as important as the memories we have of home. Here is a song (lyric) I did about my memories of our old home (and Dad) in Reynoldsburg. My Dad died in 68 between MLK and RLK. Here is a link to listen if you wish:

http://www.songramp.com/mod/mps/viewtrack.php?trackid=80833

MY DAD © 2010 Jon Hanson Lyric/melody: Jon Hanson Vocal and Guitar Dale Crockett

I used to work with Dad; sometimes he'd take me out of school

By the time I was eleven, I could use most any tool

He taught me how to frame a wall and how to hang a door

I saw how much loved my Mom and five kids he adored

MY DAD WAS A CARPENTER AND TAUGHT ME HOW TO BUILD

I LEARNED BY WATCHING HIM—SOMETIMES I SEE HIM STILL

DADS TEACH SONS MORE THAN WORK AND HOW TO BE A MAN

NOW THAT I'M A DAD—I THINK I UNDERSTAND

If Dad had lived we would have finished that house on Jackson Street

And I know of a couple of grandkids that he'd sure love to meet

He'd know his grandson serves in the Army just like his Grandpa

And maybe we could take a walk and he'd say son I'm so proud

CHORUS Bridge

It's hard to believe God called Dad home more than forty years ago

When I look back on all I've built I know I wasn't working alone

CHORUS Tag

I used to work with Dad...

====JACK: I remember when you once told me about your dad...so I know some of the rest of the story that is not in the song.

FROM WISCONSIN JEANNE: Our family farm in Irma WI and Bethany Lutheran Church with the beautiful red doors will always have a special place in my heart. ====JACK: As you may know, the church was sold at an auction and moved down the road to a farm property. It may have been the place where you lived...or close by. The owners have kept it pretty much like I remember it...but I remember the most the people who worshipped there when I was the pastor, people like your family.====WJ: Yes, the people who own it live in the place just before where our place was. I also have fond memories of you and many of the people who called Bethany "home".

FROM JT IN MICHIGAN: My memory is not as far back as yours but it sure lives in my heart. There is no place like Keego Harbor. It has produced some of the most important people in my life! (Of course that extends to the Keego annex (W.B.)====JACK: Keego Harbor is one of those places known for the people who have lived there. Even now, as in the past, Keego had character...and characters.

FROM GO BLUE IN OHIO: WINNING WORDS has taken on a life of its own, as it were. For a very long time now (when did you begin this effort?), WW has served as a continuing source of engagement both for mind and heart. It is certain that your readers, family and friends alike, have come to anticipate WW as a regular and most valuable form of soul food, sustaining and encouraging all of us to live on in ways meaningful and helpful to others. Whatever your initial intent with the first daily "publication" of WINNING WORDS, your enterprise has proven the highest friendship to many.====JACK: Winning Words got its start in 1992 with the gift of a computer disc from Daughter Jeanne. It was full of positive messages. I began sharing a few of them with family and friends...who suggested that I forward them to others. Slow, but sure, it grew. It now numbers about 400 who receive them. I post some responses (anonymously) on a blog. An internet "newspaper," West Bloomfield Patch, also posts them. One of the reasons I enjoy getting up at 5 am, is that I can sit down at my computer and set out the day's words. I call the people who receive them...C-WOW, my Congregation WithOut Walls.

FROM MOLINER JT: The Teske "Farm". Long time gone but the memories will last forever. Started today making the John Deere road 3 lanes each way. This is progress !====JACK: There were fewer cars and trucks in "those" days. During WW 2, Midvale Dairy even used some horses to pull their milk wagons

====JT: Yes- We sold milk and some cream to them. The Blood Bank now sits on their spot. (16th St) ====JACK: So....you know how to milk a cow? I never learned that skill.

 FROM BLAZING OAKS: My oldest son John had a terrible time celebrating Christmas, when we no longer traveled to Moline, and Grandma Blaser's house. 2041 - 13th Street will always be a revered home to the Blasers, Bolms, and Oaks' families, and now I dare say, my family looks to "home" at the Oaks place, where we have all gathered for Thanksgiving for so many years, and most other Holidays, as well. Wonderful memories!! There truly is "no place like home", be it ever so humble....how thankful we are to be snug and cozy and safe inside, where love abounds!!====JACK: Do you remember the book, "Giants in the Earth?" The Norwegian immigrant family sought to make a home in the Dakota Territory, in spite of poverty, hunger, loneliness, locusts and snowstorms. As I recall, they lived in a house made of sod. I like what Edgar Guest wrote..."It tales a heap o' livin' in a house t' make it home."

 FROM MW IN ILLINOIS: Now don't fall off your chair! with me replying! But this brought back a childhood memory, as a young girl, my family lived about 1/2 a block from the Lake Michigan lakefront in Waukegan. My older brother & sister would take my other sister & me and spend time on the beach.

Unknown to us,one day, there had been an oil spill, & guess who swam into it? My sister Alice & I. Mama was so mad, it took about a week to get rid of the oil & the smell. At that time we both had long hair past our shoulders.====JACK: Today, parents would "sue" over such an incident. Your mom probably said that you should know better than to swim in oily water. Times change.

Wednesday, February 26, 2014

Jack's Winning Words 2/26/14

"Never ask, 'Can I do this?' Ask instead, 'How can I do this?'" (Dan Zadra) JFK had been President for only 15 minutes when he said these electrifying words, "Ask not what your country can do for you; ask what you can do for your country." The Peace Corps was one result. Every so often a country, an organization, a person needs a "We/I Can Do It" jolt Is there some challenge you see "out there" that needs doing?   ;-) Jack

   FROM LP IN PLYMOUTH: An interesting week of WW. Drowning at work lately. Just taken on more than I can do I think. To keep from spinning my wheels I try focusing on the top 3 things that I can do that day. Since can't isn't an option I guess this is my how.====JACK: It seems that in today's work world, fewer people are being called up to do more work. As I said to a friend yesterday..."You're not Superman!" You're not Wonder Woman, either. Prioritizing is a good way of answering the "how" question.====LP: My problem is when the priority of today doesn't help me prepare for the priority of tomorrow. Clearly I can look ahead. But to borrow an expression of a colleague sometimes we are just putting out fires. One day at a time... ====JACK: I wonder if that's how Obama feels

while sitting in the Oval Office. But then he goes upstairs to his family.
At the end of the day, close the office door and go home.

FROM HONEST JOHN: Sometimes the "How" question can lead to the
conclusion "I can't.".   As in "How can I be God?". Of course, some fools
have reasoned that they could (Stalin, Hitler, Koch brothers) and have
failed miserably.====JACK: One of the pitfalls of positive thinking is to
believe that "I can do anything, if I just put my mind to it." I've always
liked the story of Archimedes. Some things make sense in the abstract,
but then reality comes into play.

FROM TARMART REV: Would welcome "some challenge" over "challenges"
. . . but will start with one today . . . "I'm going to get out of
bed!"====JACK: Isn't it a blessing that most of us don't even have to ask,
"How can I get out of bed?" We just do it automatically. A friend of
mine, with ALS, is now getting a machine which will allow him to
communicate with a synthesized voice. It's not the same as the voice you
and I use (and take for granted), but he and his family rejoice at the
invention.====REV: We are truly blessed with helps that ease formerly
complicated lives of many years ago . . . from hearts to limbs, we are
greatly blessed.

FROM IKE AT THE MIC: A pot hole repair mixture,that could be
dispensed out of an attached receptacle to the salt trucks or school buses
when available....Just "thinkin"====JACK: Evidently you've seen (or hit) a
pothole, or two, or more. I know that I have. How about a type of road
construction which would make potholes impossible to form? Put on your

"thinking cap."====IKE: I've thought of that already & my conclusion is that your suggestion requires 3 things: 1. Money   2. Top notch competent engineers   3. Honest non-corruptible politicians That's much more difficult & time consuming to achieve that an effective pot hole repair system to solve an immediate problem,but it never hurts to hope & dream..

FROM GOOD DEBT JON: I've been asking the second part of this question often lately. "How, can I do this?" It seems everything (career/hobby wise) I have done in the past has prepared me for the task at hand. I am amazed at how my past failures and lukewarm successes are now important skill sets in creating Stewardship for Life. Life (progress) requires questions. How can I do this? Who has done something similar in the past? What can I learn from that? Is there something about great nonprofits like; Habitat for Humanity, Housing Works, Twin Cities Rise, or DC Kitchen that I should adopt? Subtract? Add to? Have a great day Jack; I have to get back to editing a workbook.====JACK: We often build on the foundation laid by others. Most "creative types" realize that they are re-creators.

FROM BBC IN ILLINOIS: Wait a minute; I thought Eisenhower started the Peace Corps....I recall he started the student program my children travelled with at one point but perhaps my memory is going ...already?====JACK: You'd better check your memory! Re-researching my info....The basic idea is credited to Hubert Humphrey.   John Kennedy first announced the idea for such an organization in Ann Arbor, Michigan, at The University of Michigan, during the 1960 presidential campaign at a late-night speech, October 14, 1960. He later dubbed the proposed organization the "Peace Corps." A brass marker commemorates the place (the steps of the Michigan Union) where Kennedy stood. Critics opposed the program. Richard Nixon predicted that it would become "a haven for draft dodgers." I'll have to have Grandson Joe take a cellphone picture of it for you.=====BBC: Ahh Just looked it up and Eisenhower's program was "People to People" the student ambassadors travelling overseas representing the US. Thanks for helping me place a little bit of history. I was alive in 1960....barely

FROM FM IN WISCONSIN: You cannot spent ½ hour on a computer without experiencing this winning word – a win or a fix – a learning!====JACK: When I first started the using a computer, I was afraid that I would push the wrong key and "ruin" everything. That fear has vanished, but I occasionally do push the wrong key, and it often takes more than a half hour to get back on track.

FROM BLAZING OAKS: A few years ago, one of our missionaries to Haiti mentioned that they had no containers to send medicine home with patients who came to their clinic. Our AB women sent out a call to collect empty prescription pill containers, labels removed to send to Haiti. We were inundated with thousands of medicine containers!! I collected for the Great Rivers Region, and sent huge boxes of them, until the missionaries finally told us that they had several years worth to use up, and storage would now be a problem! A small thing but it made a difference to those people! There are needs everywhere in the world!! We can figure out the "how" ====JACK: That's a good follow up, showing

:"HOW" something "CAN" be done. I can just picture the Haitian workers..."Enough, enough, enough!"

Tuesday, February 25, 2014

Jack's Winning Words 2/25/14

"Sometimes you win. Sometimes you learn." (John Maxwell) This quote is the title of one of Maxwell's (more than 60) motivational books. He makes the point that great lessons can be learned from our losses. It's possible to turn a step backward into a step forward. Lincoln did that. Edison did it, too. Can you think of others? Maybe it has happened in your life. A failure is not necessarily always a failure.   ;-) Jack

FROM TARMART REV: "Something beautiful, something good, all my confusion, He understood . . . all I had to offer Him was brokenness and strife, but He made something beautiful of my life!" (Bill and Gloria Gaither)====JACK: I remember the story of a man who got up and gave a testimony to his conversion. He had been an alcoholic, and Jesus performed a miracle in his life. "He turned wine into furniture." He had won, and he had learned.

FROM HUNGRY HOWIE: Sometimes you win. Sometimes you lose. Sometimes it rains. (Crash Davis in Bull Durham).====JACK: You beat me to it. I was saving that quote for the first rain-out of the baseball season. Maybe I'll change it to..."Sometimes it snows."

FROM SBP IN FLORIDA: As per the most recent issue of Mental Floss: Steven Spielberg wasn't was turned down threes times for admission to film school Failing sixth grade was achieved by Winston Churchill. 600 rejections were experienced by Jack London before he sold his first story. There are more... Many among us who have "failed" have achieved using a variety of approaches.....Failures shut doors and open windows. A lot of praying is sustaining.=====JACK: These are also examples of persistence. When I was starting a new church by going door to door, gauging the interest of people in the project, I made 2000 cold calls during the first year. I had it figured out that I would get one prospect for every 10 calls. So, I wasn't bothered by 9 turn downs, because I knew the next one would be a winner.

FROM MICHIZONA RAY: I think failure is failure; but at the same time it is not necessarily the end. An acorn takes a long time to become the oak tree that it is by design. We too might consider the process of life in a similar way. The victories and losses are only little guideposts in the bigger, more complete picture of one's life. In this sense, a victory is truly no more significant than a failure -- both a merely ingredients of the full life.=====JACK: In the grand scheme of things, if every acorn became an oak tree...do the math! There would eventually no room for the beautiful flowers and you and me.=====RAY: That's probably why every tree is not an oak tree; nor every person the same.

FROM QUILTIN' CAROL IN RICE LAKE: Sometimes it proves you are human and not "perfect" but still ok.=====JACK: Perhaps imperfection in the mark of being human. The need for a "way out" is what makes us seek a leader, a Messiah.

FROM DR J IN OHIO: Steve Jobs... fired by Apple!====JACK: I'm thankful for the teachers who didn't "fire" me as I was finding my way through school. Maybe that's the difference between a true teacher and a company.

FROM SHARIN' SHARON: This quote makes me so happy because I think, coming from God, it is sometimes we win and God's deepest desire is we always learn (He never desires failure for us, we are the ones who do that to ourselves) so God also says "Sometimes you win. Sometimes you learn" and that's the truth of it all.====JACK: God's judgment is not like the world's judgment. He can separate the sheep from the goats.

FROM GOOD DEBT JON: I like this WW. Often failure is more memorable. Saturday, I put a solid state drive into my brand new computer (had it out of the box for 20 minutes) everything was great then I hooked up the old drive (to be a back-up) and restarted, nothing-black screen no way back. Sunday a friend at church and expert in computers fixed it, saying it blew up because I had two master drives. I guess the Biblical verse is true: "No one can serve two masters; not even Dell." This was an example of forced learning, but I won't forget."====JACK: When messing with computers, a little bit of knowledge can get you into big trouble...but without making mistakes, how do you learn. So, I still mess once in a while.

FROM DB IN MICHIGAN: That is so true! Last semester in chemistry class, my last lab (titration) was an absolute disaster. While I dreaded doing it again last week, the lessons learned from last semester made last week's titration lab a great success! Thanks for the good words!====JACK: You have proved the truth of the adage..."You learn from your mistakes!" See, it can happen, when you pay attention.

Monday, February 24, 2014

Jack's Winning Words 2/24/14

"Perfection is not attainable, but if we chase perfection we can catch excellence." (Vince Lombardi) Over 2800 athletes participated in the Winter Olympics, but fewer than 300 medals were awarded. Are gold, silver or bronze the symbol of success? In the Olympics, as in life, the reward is in the chase toward excellence. As Vince said, "Go "chase" the right thing." BTW, why do you suppose Jesus said, "Be perfect?"   ;-)
Jack

FROM HONEST JOHN: Vince also said "Winning is the only thing".   I would think, therefore, that his statement might be interpreted a tad different than the interp. that you put on it....====JACK: I think that the correct version of the Lombardi quote is: "Wanting to win...is the only thing." BTW, I'm glad that the Detroit Lions have hired Vince's grandson to be one of their coaches, because "we" want to win!

FROM DOCTOR PAUL: I'm reading a very interesting book "Who Owns The Future" it isn't a fast read, but it speaks to this issue of winners and losers====JACK: I think that it's about time to "retire" loser. as a pejorative word. ====PAUL: Unfortunately, economically, we are developing a working class that is losing economically.====JACK: Given time, things have a way of turning around. Sadly, we each have a limited amount of that product.====PAUL: Many of them become my coaches as they challenge me in seeing what I might say or do to bring about a solution to their inquiries!! 0:-/====JACK: The wise person is both a teacher and a learner.

FROM TARMART REV: Good word for the start of new week . . . chasing Perfection . . . "all I ask, to be like Him!"====JACK: Vince said that you'd be better off chasing excellence. In fact, that seems you are doing just that as you sit there at Target eating your popcorn and waiting for "customers."

FROM MICHIZONA RAY: I think it is right to chase perfection even though it is unattainable. It will eventually show one's limitation, while at the same time utilize all the "talents" with which one has been blessed as its steward. At any point of limitation, it becomes clear that one needs God. Our success and achievement is always insufficient. If it were not man would have achieved perfection by now! Paul seems to continuously talk about being "in Christ" and have Christ "in you". In Christ we find the perfection that without Christ we can do only the great things -- of which Solomon refers to as "vanity". So, let us be filled with the Holy Spirit in all that we do so that it is perfected by the Will of Him who is perfect.====JACK: When a dog chases his tail, all he gets is the joy of the chase and exercise. BTW, is the chase after excellence similar to the chase after perfection...never achievable, but always worthwhile?====RAY: I think that it is. If nothing else, one eventually discovers the vanity of one's own effort. Yet, as in the parable of the talents, one also will necessarily use all of one's talents in this vain effort. Is it possible to surrender before one even knows what one is surrendering?====JACK: Speaking of "knowing"....One of these days I'm going to use the Socrates quote: "I know that I'm intelligent, because I know that I know nothing." Perhaps you're aware of the mid-19th century "No Nothing Party" which had views similar to some of today's politicians.

FROM FATHER TIM: This was great!! You always have such great insights but this one was a homerun. ====JACK: I thought you might have said that it deserved a gold medal, and I would have replied, "I was just chasing excellence."

FROM BLAZING OAKS: I was thinking of those 2500 superior athletes who did NOT take home a medal of any color, last night during the closing of the games....so many who gave their all, but had only the experience to show for it. But I doubt any of them rued being there and competing. Imagine being included in such an elite group! They had all reached excellence in their field, but the slushy snow and ice made the going a bit rough this Olympics. I read Vince Lombardi's biography, When Pride Still Mattered" which both my athlete husband and coach son enjoyed (it won the Pulitzer Prize),   and he was a complex, flawed and driven man, but powerful in what he accomplished in the troubled era of the 60's! His quote in the book was ,"Winning isn't everything, it's not even what it's cracked up to be....but WANTING to win is!" My son took that motto for his teams.(He (John)is in the IL coach's Hall of Fame, and in Springfield Athletic Hall of Fame BTW) I think Vince was a fascinating individual!====JACK: I think of the thousands and thousands of athletes who wanted to go to the Olympics (medal or not) and were not chosen. For the true athlete, the excitement is in the participation. I loved playing ping pong, but was never picked for the Olympics.

FROM PH IN MESA:: to show his listeners that they could not attain to perfection and that they should stop trying so hard and just accept the unconditional grace and mercy of God.====JACK: Thanks for a good answer. I'm going to use it in a conversation that I have planned for today.

Friday, February 21, 2014

Jack's Winning Words 2/21/14

"Everybody is a genius; but, if you judge a fish by his ability to climb a tree, it will spend its whole life believing that it is stupid." (Einstein) Randy Best, a college grad, can't read or use a computer, yet now heads a company which helps colleges develop on-line virtual classrooms. It's especially helpful for those who can't afford the on-campus experience. "Normally," he shouldn't be a success. What is success...really?   ;-)
Jack

EEC IN MICHIGAN: Interesting!====JACK: It's also interesting that Einstein was a slow learner as a child..."Einstein was slow in learning how to speak. He also had a cheeky rebelliousness toward authority, which led one headmaster to expel him and another to say that he would never amount to much. But these traits helped make him a genius. His cocky contempt for authority led him to question conventional wisdom. His slow verbal development made him curious about ordinary things — such as space and time — that most adults take for granted. His father gave him a compass at age five, and he puzzled over the nature of a magnetic field for the rest of his life. And he tended to think in pictures rather than words."

FROM RI IN BOSTON: Each of us has a part to play. I've known some persons who I didn't give much credit until I saw them confront a task that had me stymied, and they succeeded with it. There are people who criticize others for not achieving success, when those criticized actually like their lives...as the common expression says, "comfortable in their own skin."====JACK: It would be fun to look over God's shoulder as He writes comments about certain people who have been written off by the world's "experts." I don't want to look while he's writing about me, though.

FROM GOOD DEBT JON: Perhaps the hardest part (maybe even for geniuses) is finding where to apply your unique talents to make a difference in the world. I watched several of the videos at randybest.com, very inspiring. You are correct Jack, Randy Best is moving forward the way education is delivered. While online learning is not for everyone with new technology it is possible to create a bonding of teacher and learner and still have the learner to learner dynamic that is so critical in cohort learning. With SFL I will be promoting four themes,

Financial Literacy, Attitude Management, Communication, and PDP (a written 10 year Personal Development Plan).   I have found, If a person is cognizant of these four areas it helps them see how today's actions can radically change their future results. Of course it is easy for us old folks looking in the review mirror, the hard part is helping younger folks see the vision looking forward. Success to me is being able to answer satisfactorily, Did I Live?, Did I Love?, Did I Matter? Success is when you know you have mattered in your life and others. It was Eric Hoffer, in True Believer, who said," In times of change learners inherit the earth; while the learned find themselves beautifully equipped to deal with a world that no longer exists."   What are you a genius at Jack?=====JACK: I wouldn't say that I'm a genius, but in seminary I was taught to take the Bible and try to connect it up with life. I think I paid attention when that lesson was taught. In this life, it's important to see the big picture in situations and in people. I try to compose my Winning Words with that in mind.=====JON: I think you do an admirable job with Winning Words, it's pretty evident that you have done a lot of good, for a great many folks, over a long period of time, the type of ministry you have with WW's just does not appear from an empty quiver. We very much appreciate your efforts, in my case I appreciate that you make me think.=====JACK: I occasionally get a message, "Please remove me from your mailing list."=====JON: So does the Pope... Not everyone appreciated Gandhi either

FROM DAIRYLAND DONNA: LOVE this quote! What success is not, is the ability to score high on standardized tests like politicians seem to think. So so hard these days for kids who do not do well on tests. Didn't used to be this way. The ability to help kids feel successful has been taken away from teachers. Sad. ;o(====JACK: Today's quote is based on a cartoon which relates to your comment about standardized tests. The cartoon shows a monkey, a penguin, an elephant, a fish, a seal and a dog. The teacher is saying to them, "To be fair, everybody has the same exam. Please climb that tree."----DONNA: All I can say is "Wow!" ;o)

FROM TARMART REV: . . . being the best steward of that which God has awarded us with and use to build upon for betterment?====JACK: So...God has appointed you to meet Jesus, who just happens to be disguised as a Target shopper (who likes popcorn)?====REV: I sure would share my bag with him (or her)!!

FROM TRIHARDER: Perfect!====JACK: If this is "truly" an Einstein quote, it proves that he is more than a mathematician.

FROM HAWKEYE GEORGE: 10% inspiration, 90% perspiration. (Einstein)====JACK: He also said: "Before God, we are all equally wise and equally foolish."

FROM BLAZING OAKS: I HAVE THE CARTOON DEPICTING THIS SAYING, (WHICH I LOVE!!) WITH A NUMBER OF ANIMALS ONLY ONE OF WHICH COULD POSSIBLE CLIMB A TREE (MONKEY) WHICH REALLY BRINGS THE POINT HOME. AS EINSTEIN REPEATEDLY EMPHASIZED - EDUCATION SHOULD BE TO "TEACH PEOPLE TO THINK"! NOT EMPHASIS ON ROTE LEARNING, ETC. HIS RECENT BIOGRAPHY WAS FASCINATING, AND GAVE EXCELLENT INSIGHTS INTO HIS COMPLEX LIFE! AND THE WAY HE THOUGHT

AND DEALT WITH SITUATIONS.HIS PERSONAL RELATIONSHIPS OFTEN SUFFERED!

APPRECIATE "GOOD DEBT JOHN'S" COMMENTS TODAY!====JACK: A good teacher knows how to evaluate students, using more than a standardized test.

Thursday, February 20, 2014

Jack's Winning Words 2/20/14

"I haven't had a TV in 10 years. It's more fun to be with people than with a TV." (Chuck Palahniuk) Author Paula-nik is 52 today. I remember coming across some of his stuff a few years ago and wondering, "Who is this guy?" His story is far more interesting than a television show. But, isn't that the way it is when you get to know people? Think of some of the ones who are more important to you than a big screen TV.   ;-) Jack

FROM TS IN INDIANA: Isn't this the truth. Sue and I have gotten into a routine of leaving home in the morning and going to a local Panera for a coffee.   This usually involves a little walk as well.   What interesting people we have met there, and developed some good friendships - and learned a lot about the area.   The TV normally doesn't come on until late in the day, and hopefully not more than an hour or two. ====JACK: I first remember going to "Panera" when it was called, St. Louis Bread. I suppose your TV time includes Judge Judy and Wheel of Fortune..

FROM TARMART REV: Back in the late 70's I was asked by the Senior

Pastor to fill in for him on his daily 5-minute telecast, "Good Morning
Springfield" which came during a cut-away from "Good Morning America!"
. . . I remember seeing myself bigger than life right up front in the TV
screen . . . looked like the professional wrestler at that time, 300 pound,
"Haystack Calhoun!" . . . I was standing on the same spot where our
senior pastor stood, while being taped for the telecast each weekday . . .
being quite larger than he was, it wasn't a good idea . . . needed to be
moved back . . . next time I was taped sitting behind a desk. ====JACK:
Maybe that was the day Chuck Palahniuk decided to no longer watch TV.

 FROM GOOD DEBT JON: Yes, I could go a long time without FNC, MSNBC,
CNN, etc. I do enjoy, Shark Tank, and The Good Wife on network TV,
loathe most sports on TV (I do watch some football). Often being with
people is enjoyable, but reading, writing, and studying or creating
something useful is far more fulfilling for me than TV.====JACK: Most of
us are not comfortable with extremes, whether it's watching TV or
listening to politicians.
 FROM RI IN BOSTON: Offhand, just about anyone I know is more
interesting than what comes out of the TV. "Boob Tube" describes it
well. The medium is simply a means of pounding us with advertising. In
England people pay a monthly fee and get TV that's void of commercials.
In our country we pay monthly for cable TV, and yet we willingly watch
and listen to all sorts of commercials...like dummies we accept that. My
favorite features on TV are the ones where someone at an upstairs
window throws their TV to the paving below. Bravo!====JACK: You and
Chuck must enjoy one another's company...while the rest of us are
watching Honey Boo Boo.

FROM MOLINER JT: Pastor Dan still,at 42, doesn't have a TV. He does "peek" at ours from time to time. ====JACK: How does he do with the 10 Commandments?

FROM BLAZING OAKS: I DON'T WATCH TV ALL DAY, BUT I'D HATE TO BE WITHOUT IT...LOVE TO WATCH THE BALLGAMES, GAME SHOWS (JEOPARDY, WHEEL OF FORTUNE) OLD MOVIES AT TIMES AND RIGHT NOW THE OLYMPICS. LOVE TO READ, WHICH I OFTEN DO DURING COMMERCIAL BREAKS, PUTTING ON THE "MUTE" BUTTON..ALSO GET WEATHER ALERTS! RIGHT NOW ITS A TORNADO "WATCH"...:-(I THINK MOST OF US GET OUT AND ABOUT DAILY, AND TALK TO PLENTY OF PEOPLE WITHOUT GIVING UP ALL TV. AS MUCH AS I READ, I'M NOT FAMILIAR WITH THIS AUTHOR! MY FRIEND DIANE JOHNSON HAS A RECENT BOOK PUBLISHED "FLYOVER LIVES". SHE'S FROM THE QUAD CITIES CK HER OUT!====JACK: As my mother-in-law used to say, "All things in moderation." You check out Chuck, and I'll check out Diane.

FROM SBP IN FLORIDA: Thoughts" The promise of TV has been disappointing in many ways. But... it does bring us the Olympics, PBS offerings, weather forecasts and alerts, FOOTBALL, as well as Wheel of Fortune and Jeopardy! And when I think of what life could/would be for the elderly, lonely, homebound, etc.....it's a gift. As for Chuck Palahnuik, I Googled him, and as a result I wonder why after reading one of his books , anyone would read more.====JACK: But, you have to admit that having a face to face interesting conversation is better than any TV show. BTW, don't be too hard on Chuck. Read about his early life. "We are who we were." A selection of his Brainy Quotes bears this out, too.====SBP: In its recent issue, Mental Floss has listed 16 people who tried and tried again....including Bill Gates, Rudyard Kipling, and Oprah Winfrey......A lot of surprises and I am sure there are more. And I Googled Chuck Palahnuick Quotes (at several websites) and, in them, for me, there's depth and poignancy and some that leave me feeling unsettled. Thank you, once again, for thought provoking WWs and for sharing the responses. Good conversation even though its not face to face.

Wednesday, February 19, 2014

Jack's Winning Words 2/19/14

"We work to make our good better and our better best." (Team Slogan) I saw these words on a sweatshirt in church on Sunday. After the service the girl told me they were the slogan for her 8th Grade volleyball team. It's a good slogan for any organization, a church, a business—even for us, personally. Success is a step by step process. That volleyball slogan can be a "life" inspiration. Why not post it by your desk?   ;-)
Jack

   FROM MICHIZONA RAY: It seems that the slogan fits the process of the open-eyed life doesn't it? Whether it be volleyball, one in a 12-step program, or the experience(s) of repentance. We "strive" more for the "perfect" more than we achieve it. Even if I know I will never achieve perfection, it is worthy of keeping my eye on it. ====JACK: The pursuit for perfection sometimes reminds me of the myth of Sisyphus. Even the best of teams suffer losses...but, then, rise up and begin their quest again.

FROM TARMART REV: That would be a better idea than I had this morning, the best yet!!====JACK: How would you rate the Target popcorn, compared to others that you have tasted? Good, better or best? ====REV: Target has a policy of popping their corn every 20 minutes or so . . . usually very fresh and often still hot . . . haven't found any lately I like better . . . theater corn is often too salty for me . . . we have a gas station/car wash/oil change business all-in-one with a large popcorn machine inside that says, "help yourself" . . . it has been a successful trademark of theirs for many years . . . I enjoy "helping myself" often when patronizing them.====JACK: Since you're a "regular," does Target give you a special rate...or free refills?

FROM RI IN BOSTON: Some sweatshirts and tees I've seen, with the slogans imprinted on them, should be burned. The one you tell about is a "keeper". Inspiration can come from unexpected sources. ====JACK: I like it when teens aren't embarrassed to express what they believe in...whether I agree with it, or not. It's called, Free Speech.====RI: That's right. It's also reassuring to see examples of dedicated teens with positive attitudes, in contrast to so many reports we see about angry and destructive young people.

FROM BLAZING OAKS: These WW brought back a little saying from grade school days we had to memorize! "Good, Better, Best, never let it rest, until your Good is Better and your Better, Best!' Hadn't thought of that in years! That's a lifetime goal, for sure. There is always room for improvement, isn't there? The bright sun and warmer temps make for positivity weather-wise!====JACK: Mary and I received a breadboard for a wedding present. Painted on it were the words, "Grow old along with me. The best is yet to be." ...not good or better, but best.

FROM SB IN MICHIGAN: Your "Winning Words" for today reminded me of a slogan that my mother taught me when I was a youngster: "Good, better, best – never let it rest until your good is better and your better is best." Not sure whom she was quoting, but it's a memorable slogan.====JACK: You're the 2nd one who has mentioned the words your mother taught you. Isn't it interesting how the mind works...able to recall things learned as a child?

FROM SBP IN FLORIDA: The last of life for which the first was made Our times are in His hand Who saith, "A whole I planned. Youth shows but half: trust God: see all, nor be afraid." Rabbi Ben Ezra.....(Robert Browning) ....and many more verses follow....but I've loved this one a looooong time. And like "Good, Better, Best"....WW continually stirs recall as well as research.Thank you.====JACK: Browning makes you think! His poetry is not doggerel.

FROM PH IN MESA: as a kid I learned this poem: good, better, best. never let it rest! make your good better, and your better best!====JACK: You're the 3rd "old-timer" who's indicated that the memory bank is still in operation.

FROM PLAIN FOLKS CHESTER: If you are happy, you are successful.====JACK: Looking back....Were you successful in your business?====PFC: Was very happy. We did great work and our clients were loyal. There were 15 of us and we all were pals. Still see several of the on a regular basis. Successful? I'd say so.

Tuesday, February 18, 2014

Jack's Winning Words 2/18/14

"I need some positivity out of you. You fought hard, and that's all that matters." (Morgan Miller to husband, Bode) Bode Miller had expected to do better in this year's Olympics slalom and was expressing frustration to his wife. Sometimes a spouse has a way of putting things into proper perspective. Grantland Rice originally wrote: "It's not whether you win or lose, it's how you play the game." A medal for Morgan!   ;-) Jack

FROM TARMART REV: You and I are truly blessed to have experienced our many years of a faithful marriage . . . meet so many nowadays who fail to invest in such.====JACK: A pastor needs a spouse who will tell it like it is. "You are not God!"

FROM FACEBOOK LIZ: she is a smart lady!====JACK: To know "what matters" is a sign of wisdom. I was impressed with Morgan.

FROM DAIRYLAND DONNA: Missed the meeting this morning. Had to snow blow 2 driveways and then took some time to take some snow pictures.

;o) I am ready for a little melting to take place. ====JACK: As far as this winter goes, we're ready for some positivity!

FROM PLAIN FOLKS CHESTER: Good for Morgan. I hope Bode learned from the experience. ====JACK: I've learned a few things from my wife. On 2nd thought, more than a few.

FROM OUTHOUSE JUDY: It's probably very hard for those athletes who spend most of their life with a dream to get to the Olympics and then to get there and not meet their own expectations. I was watching when she said those words to her husband and he took the words very gracefully. It's so easy to say and so very hard to do.====JACK: What we don't know is how much they've been through together. But in the average married relationship, it's usually plenty.

FROM BLAZING OAKS: I THINK BODE'S WIFE IS VERY CRUCIAL TO HIS WELL-BEING. THEY SEEM SO CLOSE, AND SHE SEEMS TO STABALIZE HIM. HE HAS BEEN THROUGH A LOT, AND I FEEL THE CONDITION OF THE SNOW IN SOCHI HAS BOTHERED HIM MORE THAN MOST MY SON USED TO TELL HIS FOOTBALL AND WRESTLING TEAMS, "WINNING ISN'T EVERYTHING, BUT WANTING TO WIN IS!" CERTAINLY THE OLYMPIC COMPETITORS ALL HAVE THAT "WANT TO WIN" ATTITUDE IN SPADES! OR SHOULD I SAY IN ICE AND SNOW?!!====JACK: Bode's on the "downhill" of being able to compete as an Olympian, but he has been a winner in many ways, especially in the wife-picking event.

FROM HR IN MICHIGAN: I watched her on TV and was also impressed. A lot different from Lombardi's quote about winning isn't everything it is the only thing. Did you see that horrible interview that Bode had to endure after he won the bronze in the Super G. It was shameless in exploiting his pain. ====JACK: But we watched that interview, didn't we? And by watching, we learned that Bode was a true human being. And later, he defended the interviewer by saying that she was just doing her job. Class!

FROM GUSTIE MARLYS: I think the Media could have stayed out of his face tho. They just egged him on till he broke!====JACK: I felt uncomfortable, too. Some reporters don't know when to quit...but I still watched.

FROM TAMPA SHIRL: That was exciting and hard to watch. We had seen where Bode practiced in Alaska years ago.====JACK: Did you ski on the same hill where Bode practiced?

FROM PLAIN FOLKS CHESTER: Mine was a great teacher!====JACK: There's a slogan...You should fall in love head first. A lot of people fall in love eyes first.

Monday, February 17, 2014

Jack's Winning Words 2/17/14

"Great lives never go out; they go on." (William Henry Harrison) Harrison's presidency lasted only a month, but he is still among those honored today on President's Day. Lincoln usually comes out on top as the "best" president, with Washington as next. But all presidents generally have some really good qualities. Do you have any favorites beyond the Top Two? Of those I've known, I like the one I first voted for.   ;-) Jack

 FROM GOOD DEBT JON: I think it was Dr. Stephen Covey that said, "Live, Love, Leave a Legacy." I say, no one of these is less important, though at first glance it seems legacy would be the hard one. When we invest in the lives of others, we have a chance to send messengers into a time we will not see. That is legacy for common folks, a president or billionaire may leave a legacy, but is such a legacy from life and love, or of simply infamy or wealth? I suppose each has its enduring qualities. The legacy of Mr. A.C. Bennett that was my father figure is one that stands out for me, he was neither rich or famous, but changed my life forever. For every famous saying of Lincoln, I can quote one from Mr. Bennett.====JACK: Your response caused me to think of the word, muse...a source of inspiration, a personal guide. ACB seems to have been a muse for you.====JON: You may be right, though I usually think of muse as coming from internal sources, I suppose I have internalized much of what ACB taught me.====JACK: A dictionary is a great help in understanding more about words than we think we know.

 FROM TS IN INDIANA: Now you've got s all wondering. You are implying that you voted for either Washington or Lincoln, but I know better. Was it Kennedy (my first) or Eisenhower? Calvin Coolidge seems to be re-surfacing also.   I'm hoping to read more on him, but right now I think he could be high on my list.====JACK: "Give 'em hell, Harry!"

FROM HONEST JOHN: In my time I have liked Truman, Ike, Ford and Clinton the best.   They ave one thing in common....pragmatic in their ways....not hung up on an ideological path.====JACK: Some of my favorites didn't win...Adlai Stevenson and Hubert Humphrey.====JOHN: I could never have voted for Stevenson he was too hung up on his ideology he thought we should practice universal disarmament and unilateral disarmament.====JACK: I voted for him because he wasn't ashamed to wear shoes showing a hole in one. I could identify with that, because I, too, had shoes like that.

FROM HAWKEYE GEORGE: Eisenhower?====JACK: Nope! As you might have guessed...I was on the losing side those times.

FROM RS IN TEXAS: Speaking of great lives that went on (and good stories about them), there's what should be a great movie (if it's as good as the book) coming out this Christmas - Unbroken. Here's a link to a sneak peek on Yahoo - http://movies.yahoo.com/blogs/movie-news/first-look-angelina-jolie-unbroken-full-patriotic-feels-014401724.html.====JACK: Thanks for the heads up on what promises to be a "Winning Words" film. Zapperini's quote: "Never give up, no matter what." Truly, a great life story.

FROM SNOWBIRD AA: so you voted for Lincoln!====JACK: I would have.

FROM FACEBOOK LIZ: reagan!!!====JACK: Did you know that he was once the President of the Screen Actors' Guild (union)? He was also a baseball announcer on a station that reached the Tri-Cities (before they were known as known as the Quad-Cities and also the Quint-Cities).====LIZ: he also was a democrat, originally.====JACK: Some people say that they vote for the candidate, not the party.

FROM BLAZING OAKS: I came to admire Truman after he left office. His bios and other things I've read about him, show a courageous and also "down-home" guy of great integrity! Carter has continued to make his life count for others; He was an "outsider" in the White House, and had no cooperation, poor guy! Like you say, probably all presidents have some good qualities...the job certainly ages anyone who takes it on!! Happy President's day (sleet and snow here...) and God Bless and protect Them!!====JACK: I chose a quote from a rather obscure President, because I thought that I should get to know more about him. Neil Johnson (MHS and Augie - Did you know him?) went on to become an historian at the Truman Museum. He also dressed as Truman and gave talks to groups, as though Truman were speaking.

FROM OUTHOUSE JUDY: So you actually voted for Lincoln...LOL. I liked Theodore Roosevelt after Lincoln and Washington. All of those early Presidents faced so much hard-ship. I believe all of our presidents have had heartaches and headaches while in office. We thank God for them today!====JACK: I wonder if the outhouses at the White House were painted white? I think that Teddy Roosevelt was the first President to have indoor plumbing at the White House.====JUDY: It would be interesting to find out. When I have some time, I will commence to find out and let you know. I'm glad Teddy had indoor plumbing!

FROM DC IN KANSAS: How about their wives? Yesterday we had a presentation by Richard Norton Smith on "First Ladies." Tonight he is going to talk about Mary Lincoln. This is an interesting slant on history. Martha Washington? Woodrow Wilson's wife? etc.====JACK: My vote for best 1st Lady is Eleanor Roosevelt. Who will be the 1st Gentleman?

FROM CK IN MICHIGAN: Jack did you vote for Washington?====JACK: Was he a Democrat?

FROM SBP IN FLORIDA: What happened to FDR a well as Truman? My folks were very appreciative of the positive occurrences during the FDR administration.====JACK: When the FDR dime first came out, someone handed me one and, asked, "Does this smell rotten to you." Some things never change. It's a blessing that we live in a democracy.

FROM TARMART REV: In my life time, I enjoyed the personality and presidential professionalism of Reagan...Nixon commanded my attention as he spoke up to the time of Watergate...Truman and Eisenhower were the fist two presidents that I can recall.====JACK: Do you ever talk politics while eating popcorn with your "customers?"

FROM FM IN WISCONSIN: Truman for me too, and the first Bush and Ford.====JACK: It's almost unbelievable how Wisconsin has been transformed from the Progressive State that it once was.

Friday, February 14, 2014

Jack's Winning Words 2/14/14

"In love, one and one are one." (Jean-Paul Sartre) The oldest surviving Valentine is from the 15th Century... "Je suis desja d'amour tanné Ma tres doulce Valentinée..." It was sent by the Duke of Orleans to his wife, and is probably where the word, lovesick, originated. Sartre's words echo the Bible verse, "For this reason a man will leave his father and mother and be united to his wife, and the two will become one flesh." Einstein, who can explain math, asks, "Who can explain love?" Can you?   ;-) Jack

 FROM TARMART REV: . . . more impressed with those attempting to act it out, even though they might not have it down perfectly!! Both the giver and the receiver most generally benefit from it.====JACK: There were those who thought Cole Porter's song, "Let's Fall in Love," should be banned because of lyrics like this..." And that's why birds do it, bees do it Even educated fleas do it Let's do it, let's fall in love."

 FROM EMT SINGS IN MICHIGAN: I like this a lot! I saved it and put it in my scrapbook. ====JACK: My aunt made a scrapbook for me when I was a child. She also gave me crayons...which I used to scribble on most of the pages.

 FROM BLAZING OAKS: I have a "thought" by Emily Matthews posted in our bedroom which to me, is an excellent insight into long-lasting love: "When I first said that I loved you, there was no way that I could know   How the feelings that I had back then would deepen and

grow---

       Now I realize how true love builds on all that's gone before,

       And I know that with each passing year, I'll love you more

and more."

Those of us who have been fortunate to have such a love, are truly blessed! And even after 12 yrs of widowhood, the memories are precious!! HAPPY VALENTINE'S DAY! I am enjoying a lovely bouquet of pink roses, carnations, and baby asters sent by my family...the love goes on!====JACK: ...and the beat goes on. The children learn from watching their parents.

Thursday, February 13, 2014

Jack's Winning Words 2/13/14

"Don't take yourself too seriously—Take God seriously!" (Micah 6:8 The Message Translation) Pr Eugene Peterson thought that some people were missing the meaning of the Bible, because they were misunderstanding words. So, he translated the words in a way that related to modern thinking. I have 13 different translations of the Bible in my library. But "the only Gospel some folks read is the Gospel according to you."   ;-) Jack

FROM BILLY THE KID: Amen!====JACK: When God "speaks," he's not kidding around.

FROM TARMART REV: As the old preacher shouted from behind his pulpit,

"The King James Version was good enough for the Apostle Paul!! So, it's good enough for me!! Praise, God!!"====JACK: I remember when the Revised Standard Version was published as a new translation of the King James Bible. A Bible-Belt pastor stood in his pulpit with a blowtorch and actually burned a copy of the RSV as a protest. ====REV: I'd bet Southern Baptist or Pentecostal/Holiness (sure could have been A/G in "them there" days!).====JACK: I'm sure it wasn't a Lutheran, because Lutheran scholars were involved in the translating process.====REV: I recall that fact . . . we had a contributing scholar with the NIV . . . a professor of mine at Central Bible College in Springfield, Missouri by the name of Stanly Horton . . . rated high on the list of those quite knowledgeable of the Hebrew language.

FROM DC IN KANSAS: How? Isn't Peterson missing something?====JACK: As I understand it, he was trying to get the thought across, rather than giving a "word by word" translation. Maybe that's what we try to do in our sermons. I like what he's done with Micah...."Take God seriously!"

FROM BLAZING OAKS: I LOVE "THE MESSAGE" PARAPHRASE WHICH IS SO UNDERSTANDABLE. I HAVE IT SIDE BY SIDE WITH "THE NEW AMERICAN STANDARD BIBLE" WHICH IS SUPPOSED TO BE THE MOST ACCURATE WORD FOR WORD LITERAL TRANSLATION, EVER. MAKES FOR AN INTERESTING CONTRAST! AND WHO COULD ARGUE WITH THESE WORDS FROM MICAH?. WHO WAS IT SAID, "HE MUST INCREASE, AND I MUST DECREASE...?" I LOVE THE COTTON PATCH GOSPELS, TOO! AND OFTEN USE MY "EVERYMAN'S BIBLE" FOR S.S. PREP. IT HAS A LOT OF "OUTSIDE" INFORMATION AND CHRACTER SKETCHS WHICH ARE EXCELLENT!====JACK: For dependable reference, I like my Oxford Annotated RSV. The cover binding of it is coming apart. J.B. Phillips is my favorite N.T. translation.

Wednesday, February 12, 2014

Jack's Winning Words 2/12/14

"There's always a little truth behind 'just kidding,' a little emotion behind 'I don't care,' a little pain behind 'I'm OK,' a little need behind 'Leave me alone.'" (Truth Quotes) Good Human Resource people are able to read between the lines when handling personnel issues. The ability to pick up on the hidden meaning of words would serve us well in getting along with people. Be on the lookout for unspoken messages.   ;-) Jack

FROM HONEST JOHN: I tend to shy away from the term "always". Otherwise I would agree with that assessment.====JACK: I take it, then, that you've never sung the song, "Always," to your wife .====JOHN: No, but World War One Flying Aces ALWAYS call infantry in the trenches Poor Blighters. ====JACK: You made me look up, blighter...====JOHN: Snoopy was an incredible character....I think, my favorite.====JACK: Our granddaughter heard my wife use the expression, "poor thing," and asked her, "What's a poor thing?" When Snoopy sees himself as a WW 1 flying ace, he teaches us things that we might not know about that time in history.

FROM TARMART REV: Today's WW is definitely one for my archive of treasures...reading properly the various expressions before me...humor, sarcasm, etc very often come with deeper meaning...I know that firsthand as one who has demonstrated it on many occasion.====JACK: Let there be no equivocation!

FROM FM IN WISCONSIN: So needed in every relationship ====.JACK: Your response reminds me of this wife/husband conversation. He: "What's wrong?" She: "If you don't know, I'm not telling you.".

FROM SHARIN' SHARON: Good WW. Unspoken messages are tricky. They always drive me to God because above all I don't want to misread them and further hurt the person but think, say or do something that is helpful.====JACK: I guess we don't have to know every hidden message. Some people seem to be satisfied to "suffer in silence."

FROM RI IN BOSTON: Those Truth Quotes reveal some unexpressed attitudes that exist in most of us. Those expressions are somewhat akin to Freudian slips, where persons make an inadvertent mistake in speech, exposing the person's actual subconscious attitude. It seems we want to get our message out there, but not too blatantly.====JACK: Sometimes I say to myself, "I don't care," when I really do.

FROM BLAZING OAKS: These words are excellent. I forwarded them to my family! Pete Seeger, who recently passed away, once said, "It is a very important thing to learn to talk to people you disagree with." You get some unique insights if you do this! Yes, we are all unique, even if you are (were) an identical twin! You are YOUnique to bring WW to us each day!! Kudos, Jack!====JACK: What was unique about your twin compared to you? Like two peas in a pod? Maybe that saying isn't true, especially if you compared the DNA.

 FROM PLAIN FOLKS CHESTER: ... and a little resentment behind, "Have it your way."====JACK: Yes, that's another one. Can you think of others?====PFC: ,,, and a little jealousy behind, "Congratulations!"

 FROM FACEBOOK LIZ: always a lot of truth behind "just kidding."====JACK: When I hear that one, I almost always wonder if they really are....just kidding.

Tuesday, February 11, 2014

Jack's Winning Words 2/11/14

"I'll never be perfect, but I'll always be unique." (Unknown) A new means of IDing people is a "face scan." Each of us has individual facial characteristics, so a camera can scan a crowd of thousands and pick out a certain person. Fingerprints, DNA, eye scans all underscore the fact that we are unique. In the Bible we read, "The Lord says, 'I know my own.'" If you ever feel forgotten, remember...God sees you as unique.   ;-) Jack

 FROM TARMART REV: A great picture for me to pause and ponder today as I go forth out into and among the masses. "God is watching me" . . . only do that which brings honor and glory to Him and bless those he has given His life for (even though they may not be aware of it as of this day . . . the makings of a good sermon, Jack!! Thanks-====JACK: As you sit and talk with a variety of people today, try to see something unique about each one.

 FROM HONEST JOHN: And Plato is verified...our humanness which is Perfect is "Imperfected" by the world into which we are born.====JACK: Perhaps it is the imperfection of the ones conceived and born in sin that spoils the world.

FROM RJP IN NAPLES: As I have always said, YOU are uniquer than most!!!!!!====JACK: One of the unusual things about me is the ability to recall "unusual" experiences that I've had with church members, like the time you invited me out to lunch at one of your favorite hangouts.
 FROM OUTHOUSE JUDY: This hit the nail on the head. We are YOUique! If God knows the numbers of hair on my head, you know we are all unique!====JACK: A hair stylist once hired someone to count the hairs on a human head. The total was 135,168; 6,000 in a beard and 7,000 in a mustache.

.FROM PLAIN FOLKS CHESTER: Perfectly unique?====JACK: Thankfully, God sees me as unique. He'd have trouble seeing me as perfect.

 FROM FACEBOOK LIZ: LAL. precisely why i never post personal photos on facebook.====JACK: I wonder at some of the Facebook pages that I read...Too much personal stuff. But. I guess that I'm in the minority.====LIZ yes. the couth minority

 FROM SBP IN FLORIDA: "Unique" and a variety of other defining words.... For me, "Just AS I Am" sums it up....all five verses.====JACK: That hymn was written by an invalid woman who had a sense of uselessness.. A good song to sing when we feel "down in the dumps."

Monday, February 10, 2014

Jack's Winning Words 2/10/14

"Never think that God's delays are God's denials. Hold on; hold fast; hold out." (Comte de Buffon) I saw a cartoon of a man praying, "God, don't put me on hold again." The Lord doesn't wear a wristwatch, so answered prayer isn't governed by time. God responds as would a loving parent. Sometimes, "Yes," and sometimes, "No." And, "Let's wait awhile." I appreciate the Lord's Prayer..."Thy will be done."   ;-) Jack

FROM TARMART REV: Speechless this morning, Jack . . . but appreciative of your word!!====JACK: Do you really ever find yourself at a loss for words?

FROM SHARIN' SHARON: Truly enjoyed your WW this morning!!!! And think I will write them out and memorize them to share with others. Usually people tend to think God's "No" is a denial and meant to "take something away from them". How wonderful to realize that God isn't like that but actually always giving everything we need. God is good all the time, all the time God is good. Thanks, I needed to get these WW!!!!====JACK: Some people get confused when reading parts of the Bible, but there should be no confusion when it is said that God is the ultimate "loving parent." God's children are truly blessed.

FROM OUTHOUSE JUDY: These words are some of my favorites! I wonder if Comte de Buffon was the same count who's last name became a new word: Buffoon. Perhaps not. But his words are so very true. In this fast paced "want it now" world, there are times we just have to sit back and wait. God knows what we need and it's not always what we want.====JACK: Comte de Buffon was anything but a buffoon. Besides that, the word, buffoon, has its origin long before Buffon was born. You're right, tho, in saying that "instant gratification" is a sign of the times.

FROM BLAZING OAKS: It's hard to be patient, or have hope when you've prayed a very long time about something that is dear to your heart, but what choice do you have, really? You just have to trust that for some reason that particular petition isn't God's will for whatever reason. We can't see WHY it wouldn't be within His will, but we don't know everything! Keep holding on...! Good reminder today, of who's ultimately in charge.====JACK: I do more than appreciate the petition..."Thy will be done." I depend on it. Martin Luther explained the petition this way: "The good and gracious will of God is surely done without our prayer, but we ask in this prayer that it may be done also among us."

FROM JT IN MINNESOTA: David passed away on January 25th. I am still a bit overwhelmed and trying to keep up with things I need to do.   Seems like the winning words have fit my occasions very well during this change in my life.====JACK: Keep doing what you did in the days before the 25th...One day at a time! You lived the "care" in care-giver. We continue to remember you in prayer.

FROM JR IN ANDOVER: The "Blind boys of Alabama" sing "Holdin' on! Holdin' on!".====JACK: I'll have to see if good old Youtube can come through for me. (PAUSE) I was only able to pull up a few bars of the song, but I did reads the lyrics....Interesting!

Friday, February 07, 2014

Jack's Winning Words 2/7/14

"There comes a time when you have to choose between turning the page and closing the book." (Josh Jameson) Sometimes "closure" is difficult. Perhaps a disappointment in life...a family matter, a job change, a death...How do you bring closure, or as in The Field of Dreams, how do you "ease the pain?" Every book has an ending...to be remembered or to be forgotten. In fact, there's a library out there.   ;-) Jack

FROM MK IN MICHIGAN: Beautiful way to look at life. Thank you, I needed that this morning. ====JACK: Some people need a cup of coffee to begin the day. I start off the morning by sending out my Winning Words, like the sower sowing the seeds.

FROM MICHIZONA RAY: Temporality is probably one of our most regular and daily challenges. Things we don't like, seem to last longer than we would prefer; and that which we do like, seems to end too soon. There is a season for all things, and all things a season...as it is written. Everyone and everything born owes a death, and just as in yesterday's WW theme, "acceptance" brings me some peace with its understanding -- even though I experience difficulty with accepting the timing. In the end, what value is a "legacy" to the dead? Is it simply a wish to exist in a library or memory beyond one's own season? There is always something of greater significance happening in the world than the entries of my life chapters. Someone is having heart surgery today, there is a funeral, a baby born, a decision to start something significant, and a decision to surrender.a wish for control of something beyond one's capacity, and more...so, we have eternity where the the book is always open!====JACK: Is "temporality" a word of your creation? If so, it's a good one. It reminds me of the Ecclesiastes message that there is a time (and an end) for everything. One morning, when my mother-in-law was in a nursing home, she was told that her room partner had died during the night. Her response was, "Here today, gone tomorrow." That's reality...like it, or not.

FROM TRIHARDER: Yes! There is a book that continues and continues and I should be finishing. ... But, that another story (so to speak) ====JACK: It's sad when someone who holds 'em doesn't know when to fold 'em. I hope that I know when to fold 'em...and not have to have someone tell me. We don't know what the future holds. My step-father used to pass out a card to people which read..."FORGET ABOUT YESTERDAY, PLAN A LITTLE BIT FOR TOMORROW, AND LIVE LIKE HELL TODAY."

FROM TL IN HOUSTON: Jack, on this, my last day at my current job position, and the beginning of a new position within the company tomorrow, I give glory to the Father God Almighty who speaks through you.====JACK: I looked about a job change as a calling. There's a hymn which begins, "God calling, Yet shall I not hear...?" Best wishes as you answer "His" call.

 FROM TARMART REV: . . . in some respect we are closing the door today on this week's postings with Jack's Winning Words . . . if you are like me with sermons preached, posting posted and articles read and worth keeping, the library (or archives as I call it) becomes a great resource center for another opportunity to build upon and share from what was formerly presented. It has been good for me to never lock that door. ====JACK: I'm already planning next week's WWs. If you're like me, when one door closes, I look for another one to open, hoping to experience something exciting.====REV: True as well...I've had my share as well, even wondering if there might be one or more in store before I leave Planet Earth!====JACK: Speaking of leaving Planet Earth, have you ever sung this song?

This world is not my home I'm just a passing through

My treasures are laid up somewhere beyond the blue

The angels beckon me from heaven's open door

And I can't feel at home in this world anymore

Oh Lord you know I have no friend like you

If heaven's not my home then Lord what will I do

The angels beckon me from heaven's open door

And I can't feel at home in this world anymore

 FROM PLAIN FOLKS CHESTER: Sometimes, when you close a book, a door opens.===JACK: You've been reading the Yogi "Quote Book" again.

MILTON BERLE: "If opportunity doesn't knock, build a door"

FROM OUTHOUSE JUDY: A few of our doors won't open...they're frozen shut. However, I know what's behind them....it's always interesting to look behind locked doors...sometimes it's fun and sometimes it's downright scary.====JACK: Did you know??? Half moon and star cutouts in outhouse doors are mainly used in lighting the outhouse itself. This however dates back to Colonial age whereas not all individuals are capable of reading. The half moon cutout was intended mainly for women while the star cutout is for male.====JUDY: Yep, it's in one of my Outhouse Books. The holes for the moon and the star also let out some of the odor. They usually faced the outhouses toward the winds. Aren't you glad we don't have to use those outhouses now? There is a program on now about Alaska. Most Alaskans use outhouses!

FROM CWR: You return to Michigan...............====JACK: Is that turning the page, or closing the book?

FROM SHARIN' SHARON: My great dilemma is whether to not close the book because if I do it too soon and without having achieved any understanding, I may be doomed to repeat a chapter and thereby suffer greatly once again from my mistakes. It kind of all depends whether the past stays in the past or whether it keeps coming up to haunt oneself.====JACK: Sometimes it means putting a bookmark in the place and coming back to that page when you're up to continuing. Time can be a healer.

Thursday, February 06, 2014

Jack's Winning Words 2/6/14

"Correction does much, but encouragement does more." (Goethe) I was surprised to learn that Goethe was home schooled. Besides being taught the basics, he also learned to appreciate dancing, fencing, good books and puppet shows. You see—he was more than just an adult philosopher. Most of us are more than what people see on the outside. If you were to reveal an "unknown" about yourself, what would that be?   ;-) Jack

FROM DOCTOR PAUL: I have very unusual friends!====JACK: As I wrote to Judy, LMTA.

FROM TARMART REV: . . . no longer, "unknown"!====JACK: What are the indicators that you are known by the shoppers and employees of Target and Walmart?

====REV: . . . repetitiously being there in the same seat and generally the same time, always greeting the same persons and new ones as well with eye contact, a smile and a greeting that hopefully makes them walk away feeling appreciated for who they are and a desire to renew that same feeling the next time we meet . . . I meet many new friends this way and enjoy their compliments and graciousness towards me as well . . . ====JACK: Some people might mistake you for the "official" store greeter.

FROM ME IN NEWPORT BEACH: I like Christmas lights and decorations...I am sure not surprising to you.====JACK: Your "growing up home" was a standout in the neighborhood at Christmastime. Even your Christmas tree had to have each light positioned just so. Did you inherit the meticulous gene?

FROM BLAZING OAKS: Outwardly gregarious, social, upbeat, a "leader"...but really "close" to only family and a few friends....Goethe is so right, in rearing children, or in the work place, encouragement works so much better than "correcting". Most of us learn this through experience! :-)====JACK: Someone I know was talking to a friend about the friend's "gregarious" husband and said, "It must be a barrel of laughs around your house." She just rolled her eyes. I'm sure that this doesn't apply to you.

FROM GOOD DEBT JON: Few people would know I have generally given up on politics after reaching total apathy for both major parties. Not monitoring politics has given me new life and peace of mind. You can miss FOX News or MSNBC for 6 months turn it on and the narrative is pretty much the same. "Fox: You'll never believe what the Obama Administration has done now, etc. or MSNBC: Tea Party Extremists block, _____blah, blah, blah..."====JACK: I didn't know that...but I do know that you are busy with other things, like trying to develop a program that will raise funds for someone in need.

FROM PH IN MESA: I am stunning handsome on the inside!====JACK: Ooh! I just ate my supper.

FROM KF IN MICHIGAN: I am a very tall person on the inside :
)====JACK: No wonder so many people look up to you.

Wednesday, February 05, 2014

Jack's Winning Words 2/5/14

"Good morning...Let the stress begin!" (Office Sign) Recently I saw that sign on an office wall. Yes, it's only Wednesday, but are you longing for TGIF? I saw an article: "4 Ways To Handle Stress." #1—Give yourself a positive pep-talk. #2—Take a few deep breaths, or walk away for a minute or two. #3—List some things you'd rather be doing. #4—Change your position or something in the room. What helps you?   ;-) Jack

 FROM LP IN PLYMOUTH: How does thinking about what you'd rather be doing lessen stress? Maybe it depends on the cause of the stress. I guess for me #1 or #2 sort of help but I've not (consciously) tried #4. Always good to get a new trick for the bag ====JACK: Getting an e-mail from a friend is a good stress reliever for me. It gives the mind a new direction.====LP: I'll have to make a note to read your blog for the day and see if others post their best bets. Btw does #2 include prayer?====JACK: I kept these letters on the edge of my desk facing my chair...D.F.T.P. Don't Forget To Pray. I got the idea from a successful businessman who said that he would pray before making important decisions. I now have those initials posted by my computer.

 FROM TL IN HOUSTON: Your daily inspiration!====JACK: For me, it's the responses I get...from people like you.

FROM TARMART REV: A bag of popcorn at Target, looking for and visiting with a good friend like yourself, Jack!!====JACK: Do you keep a separate bag for those who stop by, or do you let them dig into yours? BTW, Who has the best popcorn, Target or Walmart?====REV: ...they dig into mine, often taking a hand full...Target makes it a policy of freshly popping theirs every 20 minutes or so...smell of hot popped corn draws folks over to it...they win my vote for the best.====JACK: Do you keep a hand sanitizer bottle on the table?

FROM TS IN INDIANA: Blow My Top!====JACK: You seem like such a calm and peaceful individual. It guess Mount St. Helens seemed calm and peaceful, too, before it blew its top in 1980.

FROM RI IN BOSTON: The humor borne in that office sign should be enough to deflate a lot of the stress.====JACK: Architectural offices that I've visited often seemed like peaceful places, but I'm sure that there were times when that was not so.====RI: In the normal course of the work the office was quite calm and high-spirited. Deadlines for putting documents out for bidding created the most stress. At Y's office it was pandemonium when he would come into the drafting room a day or two before the due date and say, "I want to change..." and no one was about to object. Computer drafting today makes it easier to deal with changes like that.

FROM MICHIZONA RAY: Stress is part of our natural alert system that warns us in circumstances that may be dangerous to the preferable state of our physical existence (walking in the street and hearing a car horn. Stress motivates a behavior that serves to eliminate the stress). Distress is a result of our personal responses to situations (wishing it were Friday while knowing it is not, or wishing another was different than (s)he actually is, etc.). In other words, distress is when we wish things might be different then they actually are; yet we choose this fantasy, which isn't true. This contrast distinguishes "reality" from "truth". Acceptance of our circumstances first, is the best way to relieve distress...and this ain't easy! If one thinks just a little deeper about acceptance (peace) versus non-acceptance (distress), one can see how the latter parallels self-idolatry, self-importance, selfishness, and the like -- it is no wonder that the fruit of such things is distressful! ====JACK: A tee-shirt reads: 2 BLESSED 2 B STRESSED.

FROM WATERFORD JAN: If rational action can't solve or get rid of the stress, I try to cope with the stress as decently as possible. When I remember that there's help I should have sought before I tried to deal with the stress, I ask God to help me and then keep on keepin' on. ====JACK: I saw a cartoon showing someone praying: "God, don't put me on hold, again." Like a good parent, God doesn't always give us what we want right away.

FROM DAIRYLAND DONNA: Spring!====JACK: Probably my favorite season. New life!

FROM BLAZING OAKS: Ha! I bought that sign for daughter Sarah when she was assoc. Dir. of American Hospital Association in Chicago. It's a good one. Even that sense of humor would help to dispel some stress! A recent email intoned "No amount of guilt can change the Past, and no amount of worrying can change the Future". So that just leaves the Present to deal with, and with prayer and peaceful assurance, we soldier on....a sense of humor often helps save the day!====JACK: Soldier on! Now, there's an expression that I haven't heard in a long, long time. Some pastors do not use "soldier" hymns, because they want to promote peace. "Onward, Christian Soldiers," for example. You probably know of others.

 FROM FACEBOOK LIZ: quiet time.====JACK: We used to have a guy in the office where I once worked who was a whistler. He was pretty good and tried to imitate Elmo Tanner. You can listen to Elmo do "Heartaches" on Youtube.

 FROM CK IN THE AIR: Sometimes just your words in the morning ! Thanks for taking the time Jack ! Have a great day!====JACK: Are you permitted to hang any signs in "your office?"

 FROM BBC IN ILLINOIS: Stuck (next to a very very large person with luggage who was sleeping on the el this morning) but thankful for a seat at all...I began reading digital Sports Illustrated. In any case, I read the pairs figure skating article about ice dancing and discovered that Bloomfield Michigan is the epicenter of the sport and has been so for quite some time. I had no idea. Wonder if you've ever seen a practice? ====JACK: Yes, Meryl Davis, the ice dancer, lives in the same community, West Bloomfield, where I live. And Charlie White lives close by, too. Several gold medal figure skaters have trained in the area. I've seen some practices, but not fesaturing "stars" of the sport.

FROM MOLINER JT: It's difficult to handle stress with 6.2 more inches of snow last night. I can only watch as Max shovels. She loves it. Anyway that's what she tells me.====JACK: You probably shoveled your share when you lived on the farm, or did you use the John Deere?

FROM JE IN MICHIGAN: What I do is do the task/assignment that I least want to do. Then the stress dissipates because I've gotten over the big issue. I'm working on one right now. Not only is this one hard to tackle, it's vague and involves LOTS of people. I'm trying not to cause work for others and just handle it. When it's done, I'll take the deep breaths.====JACK: Sometimes it's good to let something simmer... unless simmering is used as an excuse to put the stress-producing task off, hoping that it will go away..

FROM OUTHOUSE JUDY: There are two things I do when stress hits: give it to God, and clean. ====JACK: You're a combination of Martha and Mary.

FROM IKE AT THE MIC: Avoiding "stressed & depressed people" & mingling with OPTIMISTIC ones..====JACK: If you ever want to help effect change in this world, you have to mingle with all kinds. But, you're right...mingling with the stressed can be stressful.

Tuesday, February 04, 2014

Jack's Winning Words 2/4/14

"Don't be so humble. You're not that great." (Golda Meir) This is a typical Golda quote. Another..."You never find a better sparring partner than adversity." Born in the Ukraine, she grew up in Milwaukee. Meir became Israel's first woman leader in 1969. 45 years later, the USA is still thinking about having a female president. Golda was humble, and she was great. She was "The Iron Lady" years before Thatcher.   ;-) Jack

FROM HAPPY TRAILS IN NOVA SCOTIA: A Ford colleague of mine in the late 70s had a poster of Golda displayed in her office at WHQ...the text on it said, "Yes, but can she type?"====JACK: I once asked Mary Barra if she'd be willing to serve as Youth Leader at the church I was serving. She would have done that, except that her work at GM didn't allow her the time.

FROM TARMART REV: Remember both well . . . I'm ready again for such a leader, either a man or a woman of that stature . . . "humble and great"!!====JACK: Do you have any female pastors in leadership positions in the AG Church?====REV: We do...both on the younger side (most everyone any more is on the younger side of me)...one is a licensed pastor who assists her husband with our worship and the other is a precious young single lady pastor who heads up our world and home missions outreach and our outreach to the Somalian community here in the Willmar area.====JACK: I was thinking of the national scene. ====REV: Yes as well...along with missionaries , evangelists and pastors, we have an ordained regional representative who is a woman minister...a first time in this regard.

FROM SBP IN FLORIDA: My Mom worked at Smith's market "on the hill" in Moline. The Smith's were Jewish. Golda Meir was in the area (statewise), came to visit the Smith's on a workday and Mom met her! Mom was awed...especially later when Golda became such an influence.====JACK: It's always a thrill to meet someone "famous" under ordinary circumstances.====SBP: Todah!

FROM GOOD DEBT JON: Excellent stuff this morning. Love it. Have a great day, Pastor, I am off to Starbucks working on a video script for SFL.====JACK: Did you mean SFL, or SNL?====JON: Most days SFL Stewardship for Life, http://SFLToday.org====JACK: I thought that maybe you'd get the joke--SNL, "Saturday Night Live," or did you just choose to ignore my sense of humor?

FROM DOCTOR PAUL: I saw a one woman play at the JCC last summer on her life. The challenges she faced both within her country and the wars were incredible. I had so much respect for her. I wonder if Hillary is this generation's Golda?====JACK: I wonder if Golda would be photogenic enough to be selected as a USA presidential candidate?

FROM RI IN BOSTON: That's a great quote from Golda Meir, and very applicable to all of us. In the context of the universe we are all insignificant. You offered a couple of other acute observations regarding women...that at this late date we in the U.S. haven't been convinced women are qualified to be President, and that Golda Meir pre-empted Margaret Thatcher as an "iron lady"====JACK: Are there any famous female architects, or is the glass ceiling still unbroken? Some church bodies still will not also females to be pastors or priests.=====RI: I don't believe you can classify them as "famous" but there are a few women who have achieved well in architecture. Some of them got their recognition in partnership with their husbands, not on their own, such as Allison Smithson and Denise Scott Brown. Those two are an older generation. More recently there are some women who have advanced in architecture on their own, like Laurinda Spears who was a founding partner of the firm Arquitectonica in Florida. I've read that Ms. Spears parents had some wealth and bankrolled some early projects for their daughter to get her started, but she took the ball and ran with it. Her name isn't common among architect achievers but she has accomplished a lot. Perhaps one of the most recognized these days is Zaha Hadid, an Iraqi expatriate who went to London and impressed enough people to get her going. She has had a number of major commissions in Europe, and I think there's one in Cincinnati, and they're getting publicized. While abroad, I looked at some of her work, and it disappointed me.

FROM PH IN MESA: this one I love. Jews seem always to have such a keen sense of humor about the subtleties of life!=====JACK: You've probably noticed that many of the great comedians are Jewish.

FROM BBC IN ILLINOIS: Enjoyed this one; thanks.=====JACK: I enjoy listening to the song, "It's hard to be humble, etc." You can find it on Youtube.

FROM BLAZING OAKS: In my experience, average people are more apt to have low self-esteem, rather than an elevated opinion of themselves. "A person may be proud without being vain. Pride relates more to our opinion of ourselves, vanity to what we would have others think of us." (Jane Austen) I read a quote yesterday, which seems relevant here: "Many people would be frightened if they looked in the mirror and saw, not their face, but their character." Good thought!====JACK: I remember a mother telling of the success that her daughter was having in the business world   Her husband cautioned, "Now, don't brag." Is it bragging when we tell of the successes of our children...and grandchildren? Let me tell you about mine...

FROM OUTHOUSE JUDY: "Oh Lord ain't hard to be humble, when you're perfect in everyway".....great song!====JACK: Do you remember the expression, "Eating humble pie?" It means to apologize for making a humiliating mistake.====JUDY: I'm very acquainted with humble pie as I have eaten it a lot! ====JACK: Humble pie is a derivation of "umble pie," a medieval meat dish made out of deer innards (the scraps) that not many people wanted to eat.

FROM FACEBOOK LIZ: prefacing people with "first this or that," perpetuates stereotypes.====JACK: It's better than saying, "last."

FROM KF IN MICHIGAN: I just checked out "Iron Lady" again good movie....a good woman from humble beginnings!====JACK: I was surprised to learn that Meir was called The Iron Lady before Thatcher.

Table of Contents | Index of Posts

www.ingramcontent.com/pod-product-compliance
Lightning Source LLC
Chambersburg PA
CBHW080934040426
42443CB00015B/3406

* 9 7 8 0 6 9 2 0 2 5 2 8 4 *